JOSEPH:
OVERCOMING OBSTACLES
THROUGH FAITHFULNESS

JOSEPH: OVERCOMING OBSTACLES THROUGH FAITHFULNESS

Dr. Gene A. Getz

FOREWORD BY
Edwin Louis Cole

Published by:
Broadman & Holman, Publishers
Nashville, Tennessee

Design: Steven Boyd

4261-68
0-8054-6168-X

Dewey Decimal Classification: 248.842
Subject Heading: Joseph \ Christian Life \ Men—Religious Life
Library of Congress Card Catalog Number: 95-44557

Unless otherwise noted, Scripture quotations are from the Holy Bible, New International Version, copyright © 1973, 1978, 1984 by International Bible Society.

Library of Congress Cataloging-in-Publication Data

Getz, Gene A.
    Joseph : overcoming obstacles through faithfulness / Gene A. Getz.
       p. cm. — (Men of character)
    Includes biographical references.
    ISBN 0-8054-6168-X
    1. Joseph. (Son of Jacob)   I. Title.   II. Series: Getz, Gene A.
Men of character.
    BS580.J6G473   1996
    222'.11092—dc20
    [B]   95–44557
                                                  CIP

5 6 7 8 9 03 02 01 00

*D*uring the time I was completing this book entitled *Joseph: Overcoming Obstacles through Faithfulness*, Edwin Louis Cole invited me to share the platform with him at one of his dynamic men's events. The day I spoke, I discovered that one of his favorite Old Testament personalities is Joseph. Knowing Ed's commitment to being a man of character in every respect, and teaching others to be the same, I can understand why!

As I listened to Ed speak to men that day about becoming men of character, I sensed that God was answering a special prayer! You see, I'd been thinking and praying about to whom I might dedicate this book on Joseph's life. Consequently, I did something I usually don't do that quickly. When I got up to speak, I announced to everyone present that I wanted to dedicate this book to Edwin Louis Cole—a man who desires to exemplify the qualities that characterize Joseph. The men I was speaking to spontaneously broke into applause, enthusiastically verifying and publicly endorsing the idea.

So thanks, Ed, for being a man of character and challenging men around the world to reflect Jesus Christ in all dimensions of their lives. Thanks, too, for all you've done worldwide through the Christian Men's Network to lay the foundations for the current men's movement. It's a privilege to dedicate this book to you!

Other books in the *Men of Character* series:
Elijah: Remaining Steadfast through Uncertainty
Joshua: Living as a Consistent Role Model
Nehemiah: Becoming a Disciplined Leader
Jacob: Following God without Looking Back
Moses: Freeing Yourself to Know God
Abraham: Holding Fast to the Will of God
David: Seeking God Faithfully
Samuel: A Lifetime Serving God
Daniel: Standing Firm for God
The Apostles: Becoming Unified through Diversity
Paul: Living for the Call of Christ

Contents

Foreword (by Edwin Louis Cole) ix

Introduction 1

1. A Dysfunctional Family 3
2. Joseph's Favored Position 19
3. Sold into Slavery 35
4. Overcoming Sexual Temptation 53
5. God's Presence in Prison 69
6. The Pain of Patience 85
7. A Divine Mosaic 101
8. Healing for Emotional Hurts 115
9. Forgiveness—The Ultimate Test 131
10. Rebuilding Trust 149
11. Big Boys Do Cry! 165
12. Seeing Purpose in Suffering 181

Endnotes 197

Foreword

I could hardly believe my ears when Gene Getz said he wanted to dedicate his book on Joseph to me—me? Dr. Getz and Joseph—two of my heroes! All I can say is thank you sincerely for such a great honor.

I love the life of Joseph, as do all real men. His life is a living testimony to the fact that perseverance will always outlast persecution. He is the epitome of the truth that "God puts no limitation on faith, and faith puts no limitation on God."

His brethren called him a "dreamer" with scorn, but he knew what they would never learn. Dreams are the substance of every great achievement in life. God-given dreams in God-favored men make a God-blessed world. Joseph never lost his dream, and it became the basis for the salvation of a nation. He was only one man, but he was God's man.

By "one man" sin entered into the world, and by "one man" salvation came to all men. One man can make a difference for the whole world. Joseph, the Old Testament type of Christ, taught that with his life, and Jesus bought us with His life and blessed the entire world.

Joseph is proof that God can take things meant for evil and use them for good. Joseph opened the doors of blessing, opportunity, and friendship to his brothers, and because of it to the whole world.

I will never forget reading Gene's book *The Measure of a Man,* and when I heard him teach those truths it impacted me even more.

Sermons don't set you free; truth does. The Bible is the Book of Truth. Gene Getz translates it into everyday life so we can live the Bible, not just carry it.

As you read this book on Joseph's life and learn God's wisdom through the writing of Dr. Getz, it will enrich your life, enhance your faith, and energize your desire to know God as Joseph did.

Thank you, Gene, for taking the time and making the effort to give us your legacy of faith, so we can in turn pass it on to others. And, thank you for being my brother and friend in the Lord. God bless you.

Edwin Louis Cole
Founder and President
Christian Men's Network

Introduction

What three things do you remember most about Joseph's life?

1. _____

2. _____

3. _____

Now that you've focused your thoughts, check the following events that correlate most closely with what you mentally or literally wrote in the blank lines above.

- ❑ Joseph's coat of many colors
- ❑ Joseph's two dreams as a young man of seventeen
- ❑ Joseph sold by his brothers as a slave into Egypt
- ❑ Joseph's sexual temptation by Potiphar's wife
- ❑ Joseph imprisoned by Potiphar
- ❑ Joseph interprets the dreams of the butler and the baker
- ❑ Joseph interprets Pharaoh's dreams
- ❑ Joseph put in charge of all Egypt
- ❑ Joseph's marriage and the birth of his two sons
- ❑ Joseph's brothers come to Egypt to buy grain
- ❑ Joseph orders the silver cup put in Benjamin's sack of grain

❏ Joseph reveals his true identity to his brothers
❏ Joseph's father's death and his royal funeral
❏ Joseph's perspective on his brothers' evil actions in sell-ing him as a slave

If you're like most people who have heard the story of Joseph since childhood—particularly in Sunday School—you probably thought first of his "coat of many colors." And even if you missed the Sunday School experience as a youngster, you've probably heard of the popular musical written by play-wright Andrew Lloyd Webber entitled *Joseph and the Amazing Technicolor Dream Coat.* However, once you've studied Joseph's life in-depth, you'll probably always think first of his incredible perspective on pain and suffering, often identified as his "Romans 8:28" experience. He believed that God was sovereign in his life and had allowed this terrible experience in Egypt to achieve a divine purpose, even though he also understood that his brothers had acted in a sinful and evil way.

I'll never forget this lesson from Joseph's life. It's now indelibly impressed on my heart. Though I had thought about it before, I now see more clearly that the series of painful expe-riences Joseph went through prepared him for his own unique moment in history to fulfill God's purpose in his life. It enabled him to have a perspective on crises few of us really learn until we are face to face with the impact of evil in the world. When that "evil" intersects our lives and makes us uncomfortable in areas that mean the most to us, we then have a unique oppor-tunity to demonstrate true faith and the biblical truths we so easily verbalize in the context of comfort!

Join me in an exciting study of one of the greatest men of character who ever lived. I'm confident Joseph's life will speak to you at some point that is unusually meaningful in your life. It may not be a serious crisis, but if it is, then I'm also confi-dent you'll experience God's wonderful grace—especially if you demonstrate Joseph's perspective in your own life.

Chapter 1

A Dysfunctional Family
Read Genesis 37:2

*M*y name is Joseph. I'm just a young man, seventeen years old to be exact.

About a year ago, I went through a difficult experience. My mother died while giving birth to my little brother, Benjamin. Her name was Rachel.

I really miss her—and so does my father, Jacob. He's been grieving ever since. They were very close. But since Mom died, I've grown even closer to my dad. In fact, for the first time in my life, we're spending a lot more time together.[1]

I just returned from tending some of our flocks with four of my brothers—Dan, Naphtali, Gad, and Asher. I can't believe their behavior. It actually made me sick to my stomach. I was so upset I came home to tell Dad about it! Needless to say, he was upset too, but he wasn't too surprised (Gen. 37:2).

I've seen enough in my short lifetime to understand why my father sometimes gets discouraged and depressed. But that's just a small part of his long and difficult life. It's sometimes hard to believe some of the things he has told me. Since he has completely dedicated his life to serve God—not too many years ago—he has been a lot more open with me about his sins and failures when he was younger.

My grandfather, Isaac, and my grandmother, Rebekah, had their own set of problems. They made a great start in trusting and serving God, but—as Dad has often shared with me—they got sidetracked from doing God's will.

Please don't misunderstand. Dad is not blaming his parents for his mistakes—and neither am I. In fact, I had the opportunity to meet my grandfather, Isaac, before he died when we all returned here to the land of Canaan. He was a grand old man who lived to be 180 (35:27–28). And I could sense he really regretted his sins and mistakes that caused so much pain for my dad.

Out under the Stars

"What happened?" you ask. Well it's a rather long and involved story. But let me share what I remember from the many conversations I've had with my dad—particularly as we sit out under the stars at night.

"See those stars, son," Dad would say. And then he'd reflect on something that happened years ago to my great-grandfather, Abraham. You see, God called my great-grandfather out of the land where I was born. He was a pagan, an idolater. He didn't even know about the one true God. Jehovah simply appeared to him and made him a wonderful promise. One night after he and his family arrived here in Canaan—out under the stars—God promised my great-grandfather Abraham that his children would be like the stars of the heavens (15:4–5). Well, looking up at the stars on a beautiful, clear evening often starts Dad reminiscing about his own family experiences.

As I said, my grandfather, Isaac, and my grandmother, Rebekah, made a great start in their spiritual lives. Even though Grandmother Rebekah couldn't have children, Grandfather Isaac prayed and asked God to open her womb. God heard his prayer. In fact, the Lord enabled grandmother to have twins. One was my father, Jacob. The other one who was born first was Esau.

But even though Uncle Esau was the eldest, God revealed Himself to Grandmother Rebekah and told her that my dad would be the one through whom He would fulfill His promises that were first given to my great-grandfather, Abraham—that he would inherit the land of Canaan, that a great nation would come from his loins and that through this nation, a great blessing would come to all people of the earth (12:1–3). I still don't understand how we're going to be such a great blessing to everyone—especially when I look at my brothers—but I'm sure I'll understand it more as I grow older.

A Wrong Turn

Somewhere along the line—in spite of God's blessings on Grandfather Isaac and Grandmother Rebekah—they "took a wrong turn." Their first major mistake was to show parental favoritism. Grandfather loved my Uncle Esau and Grandmother Rebekah loved my dad. It was the beginning of serious troubles.

It's true that Uncle Esau was a sinful man—a man of the world. It was no secret he was very immoral. It reminds me of my own brothers—Dan, Naphtali, Gad, and Asher. But Dad's major sin was that he was a manipulator. He managed to get Uncle Esau to sell him his birthright for a bowl of soup. To this day, Dad doesn't understand why he did what he did—since God had promised him the birthright anyway, even though he was younger than Uncle Esau. But you know how it is—we all do things that are really stupid.

A Sneaky Scheme

At this point, I must tell you that Grandmother Rebekah was a big part of Dad's downfall. As I said earlier, she favored my dad. And one day she came up with a sneaky scheme to get Grandfather Isaac to give Dad the family blessing rather than Uncle Esau. Dad went along with this terrible plan.

You see, Grandfather Isaac couldn't see very well—but he had a great appetite, even though he wasn't doing well physically. One day he sent Uncle Esau out to the field for some wild game, promising him that he would give him the family blessing. Grandpa Isaac actually thought he was going to die and he wanted Uncle Esau to have his blessing, even though God had made it clear it really belonged to my dad.

Well, Grandmother Rebekah overheard this conversation and believed she had to do something to help God—and that's when she came up with this terrible scheme. While Uncle Esau was out in the field looking for wild game, Grandmother Rebekah dressed my dad in Esau's clothes and, since my uncle was a "hairy man," she put goatskins on his arms and neck to make Grandfather Isaac think it was Uncle Esau. Strange as it may seem, the scheme worked, but—as you might suspect—when Uncle Esau heard about it, he was livid. In fact, he was so angry he planned to kill my dad.

Dad and I have talked about that event. I'll never forget the warning he has given me from his own life—*one sin often leads to another.* You see, Grandmother Rebekah had to act quickly—to come up with another scheme to deceive Grandfather Isaac. She pretended to be really upset that Dad might marry one of the Canaanite women and talked Grandfather Isaac into sending my dad away to find a wife in the same area that my great-grandfather, Abraham, lived—before God called him to the land of Canaan. Grandmother Rebekah's real reason for this scheme was to keep Uncle Esau from killing my dad. Though part of her concern may have been sincere, she was really lying.

An Awesome Experience

Well, the second scheme worked—but it was certainly the beginning of a lot of trouble for Dad. But something great happened—even though Dad was running for his life. After traveling nearly fifty miles the first day, he came to a place that

Dad later called Bethel. Exhausted, he fell asleep, using a stone for a pillow. And while sleeping, God appeared to him in a dream and repeated the promise He had made to my great-grandfather, Abraham, so many years before.

When Dad awoke, he was startled. He immediately realized that God had revealed Himself to him in that dream. But something else happened. Dad—for the first time in his life—came to know God personally. He told God he would serve Him always; he would even give a tenth of all his material possessions back to Him. Of course, at that point, Dad only had the clothes on his back, but he was sincere about that promise.

I wish I could tell you that everything worked out wonderfully well for Dad after his conversion experience. In many respects, his troubles were just beginning. But God was with him just as He promised He would be.

Love at First Sight

When Dad arrived in the country of Heron, he met my mother, Rachel. Her father was Laban—my father's uncle. Dad immediately fell in love with my mom. But there was a problem. Mom was younger than her sister, Leah, and it was the custom to always give the oldest in marriage before the younger.

As it turned out, Laban deceived my father. Even though Mom was the youngest, he told Dad he would give her in marriage to him if he would work for him for seven years. Dad really loved Mom and he agreed.

Those seven years flew by because of Dad's love for Mom. When the time came for them to marry, Laban tricked my dad. He gave him Aunt Leah instead. And in the darkness, Dad didn't realize what had happened. But you can imagine what transpired in the morning when he awakened, and realized he had been tricked. He was terribly angry and very sad, both at the same time. But as Dad has recounted for me what happened, he has also warned me that what "goes around comes around." He was reaping what he had sowed when he and Grandmother Rebekah had deceived Grandfather Isaac and stole the blessing from Uncle Esau.

Laban had another deceitful plan. He told my dad to wait one week and he could have my mom too—but only if he would work another seven years. Well, Dad loved my mom so much he accepted Laban's offer.

I'm sure you can see what's coming. It has never been in God's ideal plan for a man to marry more than one woman; it always leads to jealousy. And that's what happened between Mom and Aunt Leah. To make matters worse, Aunt Leah could bear children, but Mom couldn't. That's how my four older brothers were born. Aunt Leah gave birth to Reuben, Simeon, Levi, and Judah.

Mom was dying inside. She became so jealous, she gave Dad her maidservant, Bilhah, to bear children for her. That's how Dan and Naphtali came along. Not to be outdone, Aunt Leah gave her maidservant, Zilpah, to bear children for her—since she couldn't get pregnant anymore. Well, that's how my brothers Gad and Asher were born.

What happened next is hard to believe. Aunt Leah suddenly started bearing children again! She gave birth to my brothers Issachar and Zebulun, and my sister, Dinah.

Mom had no one to turn to but God. She had tried everything else—anger, manipulation, control. In her depression and despair, she prayed and asked God for a child. And that's when I was conceived. Years later, when we returned home to Canaan, Mom gave birth to my little brother, Benjamin. But that's also how Mom died—just a year ago. I'm sure you can understand that I'm still grieving.

Enough Is Enough!

I don't remember much before I was three. But I do remember some really painful things that happened to Dad. Laban talked Dad into staying with him another six years after he had worked off those fourteen years—even though Dad wanted to return here to the land of Canaan. And during that time, Laban changed Dad's wages ten times, primarily because Dad's flocks and herds were multiplying miraculously.

Dad finally had enough. Furthermore, God made it clear he should return to Canaan. Laban pursued us—but God protected us, even though my mom had stolen her dad's household gods. Poor Mom! It took her a long time to get over her bitterness and to come to know and worship the one true God. But she finally did!

The Lord also enabled Dad to make peace with Uncle Esau. That was a great blessing since Dad really didn't know if Uncle Esau was still angry at him when he went out to meet him. Frankly, as a six-year-old little boy, I was scared to death. I thought we'd all be killed. But God once again protected us.

Dad's Troubles Weren't Over

One of the greatest tragedies in Dad's life involved my sister, Dinah. She was raped by Shechem—one of the Canaanite rulers. I didn't understand all of that then. I just heard my brothers angrily talking about it and knew something really terrible had happened to my sister.

This was painful enough, but my brothers Simeon and Levi took revenge and killed all the men who lived in that city. I'll never forget that horrible day! Dad and Mom were so grieved and upset they didn't know what to do. As a young boy, I felt guilty about it even though I realize now it wasn't my fault. But I do remember the insecurity I felt when we had to quickly pack up everything, fold our tents, and move everything to another location.

That's when we returned to Bethel—the place where Dad first met God in a dream. Before we left Shechem, he ordered everyone in our family—including my mom—to get rid of their foreign gods. He buried them and once for all committed his own life to God.

What a turning point! God began to reveal His power in unusual ways. Once Dad buried all the remnants of idolatry, no one dared pursue us. Everyone knew God was with us, and they were afraid to hurt us—fearful even to follow us!

Dad's life really changed after that. He built an altar at Bethel and worshiped God with the whole family. In fact, God changed Dad's name from Jacob to Israel. That's why they call us the "children of Israel."

Well, that pretty much brings you up to date. As I said, about a year ago, Mom died in childbirth, but little Benjamin is doing well. He's a blessing to Dad—and to me. In fact, I feel a real sense of responsibility for him. But as you can see, my brothers are still doing some pretty evil things. That's what I just reported to Dad about Dan, Naphtali, Gad, and Asher. I guess you'd say my family experience is pretty dysfunctional. In fact, my problems span several generations. But, hopefully, things will get better!

Becoming God's Man Today

Principles to Live By

Though I've used a "first person" technique to set the stage for this study in Joseph's life, I've tried hard to reflect the biblical account accurately. At times, I've used a bit of "sanctified imagination," which is necessary even in a normal exposition and interpretation of Scripture. Hopefully, looking at Joseph's first seventeen years through his eyes will help drive home the extent of dysfunction that existed in his family. It's not an accident that the Holy Spirit chose to expose us immediately to some of this dysfunction in the biblical account of Joseph's life: "Joseph, a young man of seventeen, was tending the flocks with his brothers, the sons of Bilhah and the sons of Zilpah, his father's wives, and he brought their father a bad report about them" (37:2).

At this point, let's stop and ask ourselves what we can already learn from Joseph's experience. What principles are there to guide us as we face our own challenges in life—whether we're 17, 37, or 67?

Principle 1. God specializes in changing us and conforming us into His image, no matter what our family background.

As I once again studied Joseph's family roots, I was reminded of how easy it is to rationalize our behavior by blaming parental and family influences for present attitudes and actions.

Joseph is a marvelous example of a man who avoided this pitfall. He was definitely impacted by the sins of his family spanning several generations. After he was born, he lived in the midst of a family dominated by lying, deceit, immorality, and manipulation. If any young man had an excuse for turning out badly, Joseph certainly did. He could have easily blamed his dad, his mom, his brothers, and even his sister for the rest of his life—for repressed anger, lingering bitterness, persistent anxiety, fear of rejection, and a tendency to be deceitful, manipulative, and immoral. After all, he was reared in this kind of environment for seventeen years!

The facts are, he did not blame anyone. This will become even more clear as we continue this study of his life. Joseph rose above the negative influences in his environment and, with God's help, chose to do what was right!

Principle 2. God understands our particular circumstances and He wants to help us rise above the negative influences in our lives.

It's not God's will that we get bogged down with self-pity and other sin patterns. It takes time—as it did in Joseph's life—but with God, all things are possible.

This is not to say we'll not be seriously affected by our home environment. I know some people who suffer to this day—particularly when they've experienced serious psychological and emotional trauma as children. Sexual abuse is the most damaging.

On the other hand, God wants to bring healing to all of us in all areas of our emotional and spiritual lives. But it can only happen when we follow God's plan.

Personalizing These Principles

No matter what our family background, we must take three important steps in becoming all that God wants us to become:

Step 1—Experience a New Birth

When Nicodemus secretly approached Jesus one night to find out more about Him and where He came from, Jesus startled this religious leader when He declared, "'I tell you the truth, no one can see the kingdom of God unless he is born again'" (John 3:3).

Jesus went on to explain to this very puzzled man that this kind of conversion experience is the work of the Holy Spirit (3:8). Paul underscored the same truth in his letter to Titus when he wrote, "He saved us through the washing of rebirth and renewal by the Holy Spirit, whom he poured out on us generously through Jesus Christ our Savior" (Titus 3:5b–6).

The new birth gives all of us a new beginning in life. This is what Joseph's father, Jacob, experienced at Bethel when God appeared to him in a dream. The ladder that reached from earth to heaven symbolized and foretold the coming of Jesus Christ who was and always has been "the way and the truth and the life" (John 14:6). Referring to this new beginning, Paul also wrote, "Therefore, if anyone is in Christ, he is a new creation; the old has gone, the new has come!" (2 Cor. 5:17).

Does this mean that everything becomes totally new when we become Christians? Obviously not! We don't receive a new body—a new brain, a new set of lungs, and a new heart that pumps blood through our veins. Clearly, as Jesus explained to Nicodemus, we "cannot enter a second time" into our "mother's womb to be born" (John 3:4).

Closely aligned and inseparably integrated with our physical being is our emotional and psychological makeup. It, too, doesn't become totally new. For example, people who suffer from clinical depression may still get depressed—until chemical balances are restored. Normally this takes a period of time, but because of our new life in Christ, we can experience more rapid healing. Fortunately, medical science has given us medications that can assist in this healing process—sometimes very dramatically.

Then, too, some people experience unusual healing supernaturally. In other words, we see the same dynamics at work in the psychological realm as we see in the physical realm—for example, when people have heart attacks or strokes. Some are healed completely but others suffer the consequences the rest of their lives. When healed, some are restored quickly and others gradually get well over a lengthy period of time.

What then becomes new when we become Christians? When we're in Christ, God sees us as perfect in His Son. In fact, God sees us not only as being "justified"—made righteous in His sight (Rom. 5:1), but He also sees us as "glorified." From God's point of view, we *do* have new bodies—resurrection bodies. Thus, Paul wrote to the Romans: "For those God foreknew he also predestined to be conformed to the likeness of his Son, that he might be the firstborn among many brothers. And those he predestined, he also *called;* those he called, he also *justified;* those he justified, he also *glorified*" (Rom. 8:29–30).

This great truth leads us to our next step.

Step 2—Understand Our New Identity

The facts are that we are still living in our old body—and it is deteriorating, particularly as we grow older. But, as Paul stated, "If the earthly tent we live in is destroyed, we have a

---

* Hereafter, italicized words in Scripture quotations indicate the author's emphases.

building from God, an eternal house in heaven, not built by human hands" (2 Cor. 5:1).

In the meantime, when we become Christians—no matter what our physical and psychological state—*we have a new identity in Jesus Christ.* We don't have to wait until we receive a new body to enjoy the benefits of being a believer.

Note all of the things that change when we become a Christian—which can be summarized as our new identity in Christ:

> ➤ I am God's child (John 1:12; 1 John 3:1–3).

> ➤ I am a branch of the true vine, a channel of His life (John 15:1, 5).

> ➤ I am God's temple (1 Cor. 6:19).

> ➤ I am a member of Christ's body (1 Cor. 12:27).

> ➤ I am a saint (Eph. 1:1).

> ➤ I have been raised up and I am seated with Christ (Eph. 2:6).

> ➤ I am a citizen of heaven (Eph. 2:6; Phil. 3:20).

> ➤ I am Christ's friend (John 15:15).

> ➤ I am joined to the Lord, and I am one spirit with Him (1 Cor. 6:17).

> ➤ I have been made righteous (2 Cor. 5:21).

> ➤ I have been adopted as God's child (Eph. 1:5).

> ➤ I have direct access to God through the Holy Spirit (Eph. 2:18).

> ➤ I am a member of God's household (Eph. 2:19).

> ➤ I am a fellow citizen with the rest of the saints (Eph. 2:19).

> ➤ I may approach God with boldness and confidence (Eph. 3:12).

➤ I have been redeemed and forgiven of all my sins (Col. 1:14).

➤ I am complete in Christ (Col. 2:10).

No matter what our physical or psychological status in life, when we are born again spiritually, we become a new creation in Christ. We are no longer the persons we once were. We have a new identity in Jesus Christ!

Step 3—Continually Renewing Our Minds

Writing to the Romans, Paul stated three important things regarding this renewal process.

1. "Sin shall not be your master" (Rom. 6:14). Note the larger context of Paul's statement: "In the same way, count yourselves dead to sin but alive to God in Christ Jesus. Therefore do not let sin reign in your mortal body so that you obey its evil desires. . . . For *sin shall not be your master,* because you are not under law, but under grace" (Rom. 6:11–14).

When Christ died and rose again, He made it possible for us to be set free from sin's grip on our lives. In Christ, we are able to offer our bodies to God as instruments of righteousness—not instruments of sin.

2. "The law of the Spirit of life set me free from the law of sin and death" (Rom. 8:2). Again, note the larger context of this statement:

> Therefore, there is now no condemnation for those who are in Christ Jesus, because through Christ Jesus the *law of the Spirit of life set me free from the law of sin and death.* For what the law was powerless to do in that it was weakened by the sinful nature, God did by sending his own Son in the likeness of sinful man to be a sin offering. And so he condemned sin in sinful man, in order that the righteous requirements of the law might be fully met in us, who do not live according to the sinful nature but according to the Spirit (Rom. 8:1–4).

When we become Christians, the Holy Spirit comes to dwell in our lives. It's by His indwelling presence and power we are able to live a new life. Note Paul's prayer for the Ephesians—which is a prayer we can pray for ourselves and for each other:

> I pray that out of his glorious riches he may strengthen you with power *through his Spirit in your inner being,* so that Christ may dwell in your hearts through faith. And I pray that you, being rooted and established in love, may have power, together with all the saints to grasp how wide and long and high and deep is the love of Christ, and to know this love that surpasses knowledge—that you may be filled to the measure of all the fullness of God [that is, His righteousness] (Eph. 3:16–19).

3. "Be transformed by the renewing of your mind" (Rom. 12:2).

Though God sees us as perfect when we are "in Christ," becoming like Christ is a process which is different for all of us—depending on our experience *before* we became Christians. But the principle of "renewing our minds" applies to all Christians—no matter what our personal or family backgrounds. Again note the context in which Paul described this renewal process: "Therefore, I urge you, brothers, in view of God's mercy, to offer your bodies as living sacrifices, holy and pleasing to God—this is your spiritual act of worship. Do not conform any longer to the pattern of this world, but *be transformed by the renewing of your mind.* Then you will be able to test and approve what God's will is—his good, pleasing and perfect will" (Rom. 12:1–2).

To renew our minds as Christians, we must control our thoughts, allowing them to dwell on and seek after God's will for our lives—not our own sinful desires. This is why Paul wrote to the Philippians: "Finally, brothers, whatever is true, whatever is noble, whatever is right, whatever is pure, whatever is lovely, whatever is admirable—if anything is excellent or praiseworthy—think about such things. Whatever you have learned or received or heard from me, or seen in me—put it into practice. And the God of peace will be with you" (Phil. 4:8–9).

Set a Goal

Where are you in this three-step process? Evaluate your life in light of these three steps, then set a personal goal. For example, you may know that the first two steps are true in your life. You're born again and you understand your new identity in Christ, but you've not taken step three. You're not renewing your mind day by day—at least not as you should. As you look at your own particular situation, write out a personal goal that most appropriately applies to you:

_____

_____

_____

_____

Memorize the Following Scripture

The following verse can enable you to practice the renewal process described in Romans 12:1–2:

Therefore, if anyone is in Christ, he is a new creation; the old has gone, the new has come!

2 CORINTHIANS 5:17

Growing Together

The following questions are designed for small group discussion:

1. What is the most significant thing you've learned from this chapter about Joseph's dysfunctional family?

2. Can you identify with any aspect of Joseph's family background? Would you feel free to share these points of identification with us?

3. What have you learned in your own life experience about overcoming problems from the past? What words of encouragement can you offer our group?

4. What one thing can we pray about regarding your own spiritual journey?

Chapter 2

Joseph's Favored Position
Read Genesis 37:1–11

*O*ne of the strange dynamics in family life is that when children grow up they often repeat the mistakes of their parents. Dysfunctional families can create dysfunctional families—often for generations. Abused children often become abusive parents. Adult children of alcoholics often become alcoholics themselves—or develop other compulsive behaviors. Even when the specific cycle is broken, the emotional damage often lingers—unless victims of this kind of unfortunate background gain insight into the problems and determine, with God's help, to correct the situation rather than perpetuate the problem in one way or another in their own offspring.

Warnings for Us

This is one reason why God is so specific in outlining the flaws in some of His chosen people. He wants us to avoid their mistakes.

Remember Jacob and Esau? Their father, Isaac, "loved Esau." But their mother, Rebekah, "loved Jacob" (Gen. 25:28). The results were devastating. Let's remember that Paul stated that "these things happened to them as examples and were *written down as warnings for us,* on whom the fulfillment of the ages has come" (1 Cor. 10:11).

Though there were certainly other factors that created tension between these two boys, the way Isaac and Rebekah showed favoritism laid the foundation for some rather serious consequences as Jacob and Esau grew into adulthood and became parents themselves.

Jacob's Repeat Performance

We see this played out in Jacob's life in a very specific way. In fact, the Scriptures leave no doubt as to what happened. "Israel," as he was now called, *"loved Joseph* more than any of his other sons" (Gen. 37:3).

The scriptural record gives us a very specific reason for Jacob's intense love for Joseph. This young man—now seventeen years old—had been born to Jacob "in his old age" (37:3).

Let's explore this idea further. Most parents are more relaxed and easy-going with children who are not their first-born. Hopefully, we've learned from our previous experiences.

Another reason for this more relaxed approach is that we are more adjusted to each other as marital partners and more settled in life. Furthermore, we are normally in a better position economically to give a younger child more advantages.

When all of these conditions merge, it's natural to favor a younger child—which can definitely create jealousy on the part of older children who usually have pretty good memories of their own childhood.

Jacob experienced some of these same psychological and environmental dynamics. In fact, he may have related to Joseph more as a grandfather than as a father.

As parents, we may become vulnerable in the specific areas where our parents have demonstrated lack of wisdom when we were young. We may determine we'll never repeat those same mistakes in our children's lives. But if we're not careful, that's the exact behavior we tend to repeat when other negative factors in our lives converge in a moment of crisis. Our area of vulnerability suddenly becomes our "Achilles' heel."

This certainly could have contributed to Jacob's favoritism toward Joseph. He was repeating his mother's favoritism toward him.

In understanding Jacob's parental favoritism, we must not forget Rachel. She was the woman that Jacob really loved. Joseph was the first son born as a result of deep love and affection rather than a mere physical act leading to procreation.

Furthermore, we know the happiness Joseph's birth brought Rachel. For years, she had tried to have a child. For years, she felt animosity toward Leah because of her sister's fertility. Finally, God opened her womb. When Joseph was born she cried out, "'God has taken away my disgrace'" (30:23). Rachel's happiness and contentment certainly focused Jacob's favors on Joseph.

Finally, let's not forget that Rachel had died about a year before Joseph turned seventeen. It would be natural for Jacob to transfer his love and esteem to this young son. Joseph's constant presence would remind Jacob daily of his love for Rachel, and her absence would certainly create an even greater bond between Jacob and the son born to him "in his old age."

"A Richly Ornamented Robe"

Not only did Jacob love Joseph more than his older brothers, but he demonstrated this favoritism in a very dramatic way. He gave him a very special gift (37:3). Some translators call this gift "a coat of many colors." However, it was far more than a typical garment with a few added touches of finery. The sleeves reached to the wrists and the main body of the coat to the ankles. It was beautifully tailored and decorated.

This was the kind of coat worn by royalty. King David's daughter, Tamar, wore "a richly ornamented robe"—which we're told "was the kind of garment the *virgin daughters* of the king wore" (2 Sam. 13:18). Sadly, Tamar's brother Amnon raped Tamar. After committing this horrible sin against God, his sister, and his whole family, Amnon's lust suddenly turned to hatred and he had her thrown out of his room and bolted the door after her.

Tamar was horribly disgraced! We read that she "put ashes on her head and *tore the ornamented robe* she was wearing. She put her hand on her head and went away, weeping aloud as she went" (2 Sam. 13:19).

Another brother named Absalom discovered what had happened. He took her into his own house and comforted her. The Scriptures record that "Tamar lived in her brother Absalom's house, *a desolate woman*" (2 Sam. 13:20).

A Sign of Purity

Why is this reference to Tamar's "richly ornamented robe" so important in understanding the significance of Jacob's gift to Joseph? This kind of robe is a sign of purity. Prior to Tamar's defilement by her brother, she was a virgin. Once she was disgraced, she immediately removed the robe and tore it to pieces. She no longer considered herself pure, even though her brother Absalom tried to reassure her that these were circumstances beyond her control (2 Sam. 13:20). But in her mind, she was obsessed with the thought that she was no longer a virgin. Evidently, she could not keep from blaming herself for what Amnon did to her. This should not surprise us since we see this kind of psychological phenomenon repeated today in the lives of people who have been sexually abused.

But the point is this: Jacob's older sons were not noted for their purity. In fact, the "bad report" Joseph had given to his father about his brothers probably involved some kind of immorality. Consequently, every time his brothers saw Joseph wearing this beautiful coat, they were reminded of the contrast between themselves and him. He was devoted to purity whereas they were not. We'll see later in Joseph's story that moral convictions became an intricate part of his life.

A Symbol of Position

There's another reason Joseph's brothers hated him. This was not the kind of coat worn by a shepherd who needs freedom of movement in both arms and legs. You see, Jacob never intended for this coat to be functional. Rather, it represented Joseph's favored position in the family. It was symbolic of the fact that Jacob was letting everyone know that he was planning to treat Joseph as his firstborn with all the rights and privileges—namely, that he was entitled to a double portion of the inheritance and he would be the one who would carry on the leadership of the family. It's easy to see how this would threaten and anger Joseph's carnal brothers. Even if they had been spiritual men, this would seem unfair.

Emotional Confusion and Self-Deception

To what extent was Jacob acting out his emotional confusion and self-deception because of what had happened to him in his own dysfunctional family? Let's not forget that, years before, Jacob had cheated Esau out of his birthright and the blessing reserved for the elder son. And later, Jacob became a victim of similar deception when his uncle Laban tricked him into marrying Leah before he gave him Rachel. Could it be that Jacob was still fighting a battle of guilt and anger because of his own past behavior and experiences—guilt because of what he did to Esau, and anger because of what Laban did to him?

It *is* possible since all of us have a tendency to allow this kind of psychological confusion and self-deception to cause us to compensate and rationalize. What more convenient way for Jacob to appease his own conscience than to get Joseph involved in the same complex emotional and spiritual dynamics.

Objective and Subjective Thinking

Jacob's choice seemed so rational and logical. After all, Joseph *was* the firstborn of the woman he really loved—the woman he had personally chosen. The facts are that when we combine our objective and rational reasoning with our subjective and irrational thinking, we have a lethal combination for doing things that are inappropriate. It shouldn't surprise us, because we're all affected by sin and have a tendency to deceive ourselves. The prophet Jeremiah wrote, "The heart is deceitful above all things" (Jer. 17:9).

These observations are hypothetical and may not be accurate in every detail. However, they're significant and generally accurate in terms of human behavior. I've observed them all in my own ministry to members of dysfunctional families.

The specific facts are that Jacob "loved Joseph more than any of his other sons" and the primary reason is that Joseph "had been born to him in his old age." And there's no question that Jacob demonstrated his favoritism toward Joseph in a very obvious way. His actions were by no means hidden or even subtle!

Jealousy and Hatred

It's easy to predict the results of Jacob's favoritism toward Joseph. His brothers despised him. We read that "when his brothers saw that their father loved him more than any of them, they hated him and could not speak a kind word to him" (37:4).

Jealousy and hatred are withering emotions that are devastating to human relationships—particularly within families. Generally speaking, people who resent others find it very difficult to communicate positively with those who are the object of their resentment. And this was exactly what happened in Joseph's family. His brothers were not about to compliment Joseph—nor were they going to wish him God's best.

One-on-one hatred is difficult to deal with. But the problem is compounded and greatly complicated when people are drawn together in common hatred. They feed on one another's feelings of resentment and collaborate in their actions. They spur one another on. And, as we'll see in a future chapter, this is exactly what happened among Joseph's brothers.

Joseph had to know he was out of harmony with his brothers. They could say nothing good about him nor to him. After all, he had already gotten some of them into serious trouble with their father by reporting their bad behavior (37:2). And now—the royal robe! Joseph was definitely on the outside looking in. The rejection he felt must have been extremely intense, creating severe anxiety and deep feelings of insecurity.

Joseph's Naiveté

Joseph would eventually become a very wise man. However, he would learn these lessons in the "school of hard knocks." But at this point in his life, he was definitely naive. After all, he was only seventeen. His heart was pure but he lacked the experience and wisdom that comes from growing older. This should not surprise us since Joseph was a normal kid. He may have been head and shoulders above his older brothers spiritually, but that did not keep him from making some bad judgments.

Joseph was also a victim of his father's bad judgments. Jacob definitely set Joseph up for some very difficult days ahead. Rather than helping Joseph, he was—in the long run—hurting him. Remember, too, that there is no way a teenage boy is going to turn down a royal robe—particularly from a father who loved him so intently.

Imagine for a moment that you have a number of children. All of them have given you a rough time except your youngest. He is disciplined, cooperative, sensitive, loving, and just an all-around good kid. In the meantime, you've done pretty well in life. You've saved some money. And your youngest son is seventeen, ready to graduate from high school— with highest honors, no less.

You're really proud of your son—and who can blame you? On graduation night, with the entire family present for this lovely occasion, you unveil a little surprise. When your son walks out of the school gym following graduation exercises, there, sitting in front of the school, is a dream of every young man. The sign reads: "Congratulations, son! You deserve it!" The gift? A brand new sports car!

What do you think the older children would be thinking—and feeling—especially since you never gave them anything comparable? In fact, they've sensed all along that you didn't love them as you love your youngest son.

Obviously, in a case like this, you would be demonstrating unfair actions toward your older children, no matter what their behavior. Furthermore, you would be doing your youngest a terrible disservice—setting him up for some very unhappy experiences in the future.

But there's not one of us who would blame your son for accepting the gift. The problem would focus on you, the father, rather than on your son. And that is exactly the case in this Old Testament story.

Jacob showed unusual favoritism toward Joseph. And Joseph, naturally, accepted that favoritism. In fact, like any seventeen-year-old, he enjoyed it. But in the process, he also became vulnerable in the midst of some very predictable temptations.

Two Prophetic Dreams

The Sheaves of Grain

Joseph had a dream. He was with his brothers "binding sheaves of grain out in the field." Suddenly, his "sheaf rose and stood upright." His brothers' sheaves "gathered around" Joseph's and "bowed down to it" (37:5–7).

Can you imagine the reaction of his brothers? There Joseph stood in his royal robe sharing this nocturnal experience. They saw the implication immediately. Their response says it all—"'Do you intend to reign over us? Will you actually rule us?'" (37:8). And the text gives us not only their verbal responses, but their emotional reactions as well: "And *they hated him all the more* because of his dream and what he had said."

We certainly know from the total story of Joseph's life that this dream was prophetic. It came from God. Many years later, his brothers did exactly what their sheaves of grain did—"they bowed down to him with their faces to the ground" (42:6).

There are also some human explanations for certain elements of this dream. After all, he *had* received a royal robe. Furthermore, he was favored by his father. It would have been very natural for a seventeen-year-old to have visions of grandeur that translated themselves into dreams. And, certainly, the nature of this dream and the one to follow fits the natural circumstances that were taking place in his own family relationships. Nevertheless, the dream was from the Lord—which blended supernatural and natural factors in a way that only God can orchestrate.

Though this dream was definitely supernatural, Joseph made a serious error in judgment when he shared it with his brothers. Based upon what was happening in his relationship with his father, Joseph believed God was going to use him in a special way. However, it was lethal and very naive for Joseph to share this kind of information with his brothers who were already in bondage to feelings of jealousy and hatred.

Joseph had to be feeling a lot of anxiety because of his brothers' rejection. It would be natural for him to want to prove himself. What better way to do that—from his perspective—than to try to demonstrate that God was on his side.

But it was like waiving a red blanket in front of a charging bull—in this case, eleven "bulls." Normally, carnal and sinful people don't respond well to the Word of God—especially from a young sibling who had just tattled on them and who was now trying to demonstrate that he had supernatural authority over them. Their intense negative reactions are predictable.

The "Sun and Moon and Eleven Stars"

In Joseph's second dream, the "sun and moon and eleven stars" bowed down to him (37:9). If there had been any question about the meaning of the first dream (and there wasn't), there certainly was no speck of doubt regarding the meaning of the second dream. When he mentioned the "eleven stars," the details were more than obvious. And his brothers' jealous reactions more than verified they understood the symbolism (37:11).

Joseph also shared this second dream with his father who got the message very quickly. Jacob "rebuked him," asking him a very pointed question—"'Will your mother and I and your brothers actually come and bow down to the ground before you?'" (37:10).

Jacob was shocked and taken aback by what he heard. On the other hand, he subsequently did some serious thinking about Joseph's dream. We read that he "kept the matter in mind" (37:11). Upon reflection, he knew his son well enough to know that this was not just a sign of personal ambition. I believe Jacob concluded rather quickly that Joseph's dreams were in some way prophetic.

Some Final Thoughts and Insights

Hindsight Is Often 20/20

Since we know the complete story, we can speculate rather objectively as to what was happening to Joseph. If he had been secure and wise, he wouldn't have shared his dreams with his brothers. Rather, he would have gone to his father privately, seeking help in understanding his feelings, his motives, and the meaning of his dreams. If he had, both he and his father would have avoided some serious problems.

But even more importantly, if Jacob had been wise and mature in his relationship with his children, he would not have set Joseph up for what was about to happen. Because of his favoritism toward Joseph, he actually created the environment that triggered the jealousy and hatred toward his young son.

A Catch-22

Joseph was caught in the middle between his father and his brothers. On the one hand, he was feeling anxious and insecure because of his brothers' hatred and rejection. On the other hand, he was feeling approval and encouragement from his father.

Furthermore, Joseph's first dream seemed to justify his father's favoritism. Maybe his brothers would understand and accept him if they knew about this dream. But sharing this experience only led to more rejection.

Joseph's second dream only reinforced his desire to be accepted. This time it was not just a reference to his brothers collectively, but to his eleven brothers—as well as his father and mother. The fact that he shared this dream with his father indicates he was seeking his father's continual support and approval in the midst of his anxiety. This would be a natural thing for Joseph to do in this kind of family predicament. Unfortunately for Joseph, his brothers' jealousy only deepened and he now was rebuked by his father.

Think for a moment about your own reactions when you feel insecure, particularly when you feel rejection from people you are close to. Our tendency is to try to prove that "we're OK." In many respects, this appears to be Joseph's reaction to this crisis situation at this moment in his life.

Becoming God's Man Today

Principles to Live By

It's difficult to unravel all the factors involved in circumstances and situations like this, particularly when both human and divine elements are involved. But there is enough information in this passage to learn some very specific and valuable lessons. Also, we have the advantage of interpreting these isolated experiences in the light of the total story of Joseph's life, which makes the lessons we can learn even more specific and practical.

Principle 1. As parents (and grandparents), we must be on guard against showing favoritism.

This principle applies particularly to our children who are younger. Remember, too, that in our culture we usually have more to share with our younger children materially than when we were just starting out. Don't forget that your older children have good memories. It takes a great deal of wisdom not to, on the one hand, penalize the younger child just because he happens to be the youngest and, at the same time, maintain equity with the older children.

Furthermore, we naturally tend to show favoritism to the child or children who are the most cooperative and appreciative. Once again, this is a difficult tightrope to walk, since it is not wrong to reward good behavior. But to do so without showing favoritism is a constant challenge!

Your youngest child's positive behavior may reflect the fact that you've learned more about being a good parent. Unfortunately, older children often reflect our own mistakes more vividly in their behavior.

Principle 2. All of us have factors, both within us and within our environment, that tend to cloud our thinking and blur our judgments.

Some of these problems are self-induced. They are purely our fault. Conversely, some of the factors relate to the mistakes of others. This was certainly true in Jacob's life as well as Joseph's. This is why we must always maintain an attitude of openness and teachability.

We're particularly vulnerable to making unwise decisions when we're young. No matter how much we think we know, there is much that we don't know, and this lack of wisdom and experience will inevitably lead us to make naive judgments. This is why we need to listen to those who are older and more mature than we are—even though we can all cite instances when older people have made serious judgment errors as well.

This was certainly true of Joseph's father. Growing older doesn't guarantee maturity, but it's an important factor in God's scheme of things. This is why the Scriptures use the term *elders* to describe the spiritual leaders in the church. This word refers to "older men" who are wise and discerning. However, age per se is not the only basis for selecting men who serve in these leadership roles. Paul included a lengthy list of qualifications that should accompany age—qualifications that reflect spiritual and psychological maturity (see 1 Tim. 3:1–7; Titus 1:5–9).[1]

Principle 3. All of us, no matter what our age, tend to make naive judgments when we become anxious and insecure.

This is particularly true when we sense rejection. We often step up our efforts to prove "we're OK"; in the process, we often experience more rejection especially if our behavior is threatening to others in the first place.

Remember, too, that many people who threaten others with their personalities, their success patterns, and their capabilities do not understand what is happening. They do not purposely set out to threaten or overshadow others. They do not think of themselves as being more skilled or more capable. This is also a naive perspective—and probably was true to a great extent in Joseph's life.

Personalizing These Principles

Following are some questions to help you pinpoint areas that may need attention in your own life:

1. As a parent, am I showing favoritism? Is this caused by economic factors? Personality differences in the children?

Results of my own growth as a parent? Compensation for the mistakes I've made in the past?

2. What can I do to reward good behavior among my children but not show favoritism in the process?

Discussing these matters together as father and mother is one way to avoid making decisions that show favoritism. It's also helpful to seek advice from another couple who is working through the same problems as you are, or perhaps someone you know has already faced these problems and would give you wise counsel. Communication with our children is also a very important factor in avoiding feelings of favoritism.

3. As a Christian, what factors in my experience cause me to be naive and to make inadequate judgments?

If this question is threatening, it may indicate that you are afraid to ask advice for fear you'll discover you actually need help. Try to deal with this fear by reminding yourself that everyone needs help.

4. As a Christian, am I trying to prove myself by working hard to please others who are rejecting me, perhaps because they are threatened by me in the first place?

Set a Goal

Use these guidelines to evaluate your behavior in light of these "Principles to Live By." Then set a personal goal. For example, you may have just gained insight for the first time that you have factors within you that have clouded your thinking and blurred your judgments. Based upon this insight or others, write out a personal goal for your life:

_____

_____

_____

_____

Memorize the Following Scripture

The following verse can enable you to seek God's wisdom in facing difficult situations in your life.

If any of you lacks wisdom, he should ask God, who gives generously to all without finding fault, and it will be given to him.

JAMES 1:5

Growing Together

The following questions are designed for small group discussion:

1. What insights from this study have you gotten regarding your own family background? Would you feel free to share these insights with the others in this group?

2. Have you been able to isolate some areas in your family relationships that need correcting? Would you feel free to share these areas?

3. If necessary, how can we go about correcting our mistakes?

4. What have you found to be guidelines for making good judgments in your family, in your church, in your vocation, and in other social relationships?

5. What personal prayer request would you like to share?

Chapter 3

Sold into Slavery

Read Genesis 37:12–36

*A*s I reflect on my own experience as a husband and a father, I'm amazed at the way I had to *learn* to be in touch with the feelings of other members of my family. In fact, there were certainly times when I *thought* I knew what they were feeling, only to discover that I didn't have a clue.

Whether an innate problem because we're men, or something that relates to our culture, one thing is certain. Most men seem to have difficulty understanding feelings. However, being in touch with others' feelings is not just a man's problem. I have met many women who have no insight whatsoever as to what their husbands are really feeling.

I must hurriedly add—and admit—that part of this problem relates to the fact that many men tend to be passive and noncommunicative. Most men I've met not only have difficulty getting in touch with others' feelings, but also have difficulty understanding and sharing their own feelings. This is a lethal combination.

Jacob—Joseph's father—had difficulty in both areas, and remember that Jacob's culture was entirely different from most of ours. Does this support the theory that this is simply a universal problem for men—and it's always been that way ever since sin entered the world? Maybe so!

Two Themes in Joseph's Life

The "Coat of Many Colors"

When many of us were small children attending Sunday School, we heard the story of this young man and how his brothers cruelly stripped him of his "coat of many colors," mercilessly threw him into a pit, and then without shame and remorse sold him as a slave to a band of merchants who were traveling to Egypt. They then slaughtered a goat, dipped Joseph's coat in the blood, and presented it to their father, allowing Jacob to conclude that Joseph had been killed by a wild animal.

In more recent years, playwright Andrew Lloyd Webber has popularized this theme with his modern stage play entitled *Joseph and the Amazing Technicolor Dream Coat.* Though secular, the main story line in this dramatic production is quite true to the biblical story. But the "theme" Webber capitalizes on—and rightfully so—is Joseph's "richly ornamented robe."

The "Jacob Connection"

The second theme running through this story is more subtle and focuses on Joseph's father and why his sons behaved as they did. It's this theme that produces the most valuable lessons for parents. Though Jacob's sons were certainly responsible before God for their sinful behavior, there were some very definite connections between the way Jacob carried out his parental role and his sons' attitudes and actions.

A Wealthy Man

While living in the land of his father-in-law, Laban, Jacob "grew exceedingly prosperous and came to own large flocks, and maidservants and menservants, and camels and donkeys" (30:43).

Later when he met his brother, Esau, he gave him a generous gift of "two hundred female goats and twenty male goats, two hundred ewes and twenty rams, thirty female camels with their young, forty cows and ten bulls, and twenty female donkeys and ten male donkeys"—a total of 550 animals (32:14–15).

The shear size of this gift gives us some idea as to Jacob's wealth. Personally, I believe that this selection may have been based on a tenth of his livestock. When Jacob first met God at Bethel, he promised the Lord he would give a tithe of everything he owned if the Lord prospered him and made it possible (28:20–22). This may have been his first opportunity to follow through on his commitment, considering this gift to Esau a gift to God.

If my theory is correct, Jacob's livestock probably numbered at least 2,000 female goats, 200 male goats, 2,000 ewes, 200 rams, 300 female camels, 400 cows, 100 bulls, 200 female donkeys, and 100 male donkeys. By any measuring stick, this represents a lot of wealth.[1]

An Uneasy Feeling

Though Jacob first set up camp near the city of Shechem after he returned to Canaan, he eventually settled in Hebron. However, he continued to graze his livestock near Shechem—which is about fifty miles away. Jacob put his ten older sons in charge (37:12–14).

As time passed, Jacob became concerned about this arrangement. It may appear he was primarily uneasy about his sons' physical welfare when he told Joseph, "'Go and see if all is well with your brothers and with the flocks, and bring word back to me'" (37:14). However, if we look at the broader picture, we find clues regarding what Jacob was really thinking and feeling.

Joseph's Bad Report

The first clue is in the immediate context. As we've already noted in a previous chapter, Joseph had been "tending the flocks with his brothers"—probably near Shechem—and had "brought their father a *bad report* about them" (37:2). We're not told the content of the report, but we can certainly speculate it must have been a serious violation of God's standards of righteousness.

Jacob's concern, then, involved more than wanting to know about his sons' health. From Joseph's "bad report," Jacob had reason to wonder about their behavior and how this would also affect the welfare of his flocks.

A Double Tragedy

Jacob's concerns, however, also go back several years before, when he had set up residence near the city of Shechem—where his sons were now grazing his flocks (37:12). In fact, he had purchased a piece of land from the sons of Hamor the Hivite, the ruler of the area (33:19). While living in this area, Jacob faced a double tragedy—which still had to be very fresh in his mind (34:1–31).

Dinah's Violation

Hamor the Hivite had a son, also known as Shechem. In fact, the city was no doubt named after him.

One day Dinah—Jacob's only daughter—decided to leave the confines of her own residence and to wander out "to visit the women of the land" (34:1). Keep in mind that these women were pagans. They worshiped idols and were typical "women of the world." Though we're not given specifics, some of these women probably introduced Dinah to Shechem. She became sexually involved with this young prince. The biblical record states that "he violated her" (34:2). Today in our culture we might call this "date rape." However, Shechem evidently kept her in his own home (34:26) though we're not told whether she was held captive against her will or if she was cooperative.

What began as a lustful adventure for Shechem turned into real love toward Dinah. He sincerely wanted to marry this young Israelite. Consequently, he made every effort to try to win Jacob's approval and to secure permission to take Dinah as his legal wife.

Encouraging Jacob in this direction, Shechem's own father gave Jacob an open invitation to occupy the area. "'You can settle among us,'" he promised. "'The land is open to you. Live in it, trade in it, and acquire property in it'" (34:10). And Shechem himself added to this generous offer, which indicates this young man's personal wealth—"'Let me find favor in your eyes, and I will give you whatever you ask. Make the price for the bride and the gift I am to bring as great as you like, and I'll pay whatever you ask me. Only give me the girl as my wife'" (34:11–12).

We're not told specifically how Jacob responded to all of this. However, the implication is that he was rather passive when he received the initial report. We read that when he "heard that his daughter Dinah had been defiled, his sons were in the fields with his livestock; *so he kept quiet about it until they came home*" (34:5).

Why did Jacob remain quiet? Frankly, had this been my daughter, I don't think I'd have waited until my sons came home. Hopefully, I would have hightailed it immediately to where they were and called a family council meeting to discuss how to face this crisis. In fact, I'm not sure how well I would have controlled my anger.

Horrible Retaliation

By contrast, when Jacob's sons heard about what had happened, they reacted with intense emotion. The scriptural text states that "they were filled with *grief* and *fury*" (34:7). They wasted no time in plotting against Shechem and the men of the city—telling them they would consent to Dinah's marriage if all the men would consent to be circumcised. Shechem and his fellow Shechemites believed they were sincere and agreed—but while they were physically recovering from this experience, Simeon and Levi "took their swords and attacked the unsuspecting city, killing every male" (34:25).

Rather than dealing directly with his sons' murderous actions, it appears Jacob was primarily concerned about his own status and welfare. Speaking specifically to Simeon and Levi—the two sons who committed this horrible atrocity—he exclaimed, "'You have brought trouble on *me* by making *me* a stench to the Canaanites and Perizzites, the people living in this land. We are few in number, and if they join forces against *me* and attack *me, I* and *my* household will be destroyed'" (34:30).

To be fair to Jacob, an attack on him was an attack on his whole family. Nevertheless, he did not deal openly with this atrocity, and from the biblical record it appears he was very self-absorbed!

A Significant "Burial" Experience

There is, however, another side to this story. The Lord used this event in Jacob's life to get his attention. It was at this point he called a family meeting and ordered everyone in his household to "get rid" of all their "foreign gods" (35:2). He buried them there "under the oak at Shechem" (35:4).

Jacob had no choice but to leave. He traveled first to Bethel and eventually to Hebron, where he settled permanently. Several years later, his sons returned to graze Jacob's flock in the same vicinity. We can, therefore, understand why Jacob sent Joseph to check up on his sons and his flocks. He did not trust them—and understandably so. Who knew what trouble they might be up to—particularly in the area where they had created so many enemies with their murderous act against the Shechemites.

A Hideous Plot

"Let's Kill Him"

Neither Joseph nor his father anticipated what was about to happen. Jacob's sons were not the least bit impressed with their brother's appearance. When "they saw him in the distance," their intense hatred was rekindled and "they plotted to kill him" (37:18). And there was no way they could miss who he was. Joseph was wearing his "richly ornamented robe." Even at a distance, he looked like a prince, not a fellow shepherd.

At least four of Jacob's sons were certainly still angry regarding Joseph's bad report to their father the last time "little brother" was with them. Furthermore, *all of them* remembered his dreams that clearly predicted they would at some point in time "bow down to him" and honor him as their superior. "Here comes that dreamer!" they said, *"come now, let's kill him."* Conspiring together, they decided to "take his life," and to dispose of his body by throwing him into one of the cisterns. They would then report to their father that a "ferocious animal" had "devoured" Joseph (37:19–20).

"We'll see what comes of his dreams," they must have shouted among themselves, their voices trembling with anger (37:20). In no way were they going to acknowledge Joseph as their superior. And to prove his dreams false, they decided to eliminate the possibility of any fulfillment by destroying their younger brother.

"Let's Not Take His Life"

Knowing Joseph's brothers jealousy and hatred toward their younger brother, it's not surprising that they retaliated. But they were not all in agreement as to what steps to take. Reuben, the oldest son, definitely disagreed with their plan. *"'Let's not take his life,'* he said. 'Don't shed any blood. Throw him into this cistern here in the desert, but don't lay a hand on him'" (37:21–22).

The other brothers consented to Reuben's alternate plan even though most of them still wanted to take Joseph's life. But they definitely agreed on one thing—they hated Joseph and loathed the idea of having him in authority over them. Consequently, when Joseph arrived, they tore off his richly ornamented robe and "threw him into the cistern" (37:24).

You can imagine Joseph's shock and fear as he walked into this threatening situation. In his naiveté, he must have thought his brothers would be happy to see him. After all, in his own mind, he had come to check up on their welfare, probably not comprehending his father's deeper concerns regarding his brothers' sinful behavior. Though the immediate text does not specify Joseph's emotional response, we know from the brothers' later confession in Egypt that he was extremely "distressed." He "pleaded" with them "for his life." However, they showed no mercy and "would not listen" (42:21).

"Let's Sell Him to the Ishmaelites"

In the meantime, the sons of Jacob nervously "sat down to eat their meal," no doubt discussing what to do next. Reuben—who at this point was absent—had proposed this alternate plan. But if they were not going to take his life, then what were they going to do with Joseph? What would they tell their father? Releasing him would be out of the question since Joseph would only come home and report their hostile reception. They saw no way out but to override Reuben.

In the midst of what must have been some very intense arguing, they looked up and "saw a caravan of Ishmaelites coming from Gilead" who were headed for Egypt to do some trading. Judah, Leah's fourth son, immediately saw a solution to their dilemma. "'What will we gain if we kill our brother and cover up his blood?'"—indicating that most of them had not given up on their plot to kill Joseph. "'Come,'" he proposed, *"let's sell him to the Ishmaelites* and not lay our hands on him; after all, he is our brother, our own flesh and blood'" (37:25–27).

From this suggested solution, we can conclude that Judah evidently had sided with Reuben. The caravan of Ishmaelites would be a way to get rid of Joseph without actually killing him. At this point, they all agreed—except Reuben—who was not present to voice his disapproval.

"Where Can I Turn Now?"

Later, Reuben—still unaware of what had happened—"returned to the cistern and saw that Joseph was not there" (37:29). Terribly disturbed to find Joseph missing, "he tore his clothes." Returning to his brothers with the startling news that Joseph was gone, he cried out, *"Where can I turn now?"* (37:30).

Though Reuben seemed deeply troubled about Joseph's disappearance, evidently it did not take long for his brothers to convince him to go along with their plot. After all, they could "have their cake and eat it too." Joseph would be gone— out of their hair. Furthermore, they could explain his absence by following through on their original plan without actually killing their brother.

Why was Reuben so protective of Joseph? Was it true concern? If it was, then why did he agree to the fabricated plan so quickly? Why did he not protest the sale of Joseph? Why did he not go after the Ishmaelite caravan and redeem his brother— no matter what the cost?

Reuben's concerns were, first and foremost, based on his desire to protect himself. After all, he was the eldest, and he knew he would have to face his father with an explanation for Joseph's absence. Furthermore, his birthright was at stake.

A "Skeleton" in Reuben's Closet. Reuben was already in trouble with his father. He had a terrible "skeleton" in his closet. On a previous occasion, he committed a heinous sin. After Rachel's death, Reuben had committed incest. The scriptural record states it clearly—and bluntly. When Jacob's family was camped in the region of Migdal Eder, "Reuben went in and slept with his father's concubine Bilhah" (35:22).

Though it was customary in this culture for a man to bear children by means of a concubine, it was not customary nor acceptable for a son to take sexual liberties with the same woman. In doing so, Reuben engaged in sexual intercourse with the mother of his two brothers—Dan and Naphtali.

Another Incident of Passivity. Jacob's reaction to this event gives us more insight into his approach to parenting. All we read is that he *"heard of it."* However, there's no evidence he did anything specific about it at the time. But we know Jacob never forgot it! Years later when he pronounced his final blessing upon his sons, he stated the following: "'Reuben, you are my firstborn, my might, the first sign of my strength, excelling in honor, excelling in power. Turbulent as the waters, you will no longer excel, for you went up onto your father's bed, onto my couch and defiled it'" (49:3–4).

Though Jacob had evidently said very little to Reuben about this matter when it happened, he certainly said enough for the eldest son to know he was already in trouble. He *knew* his father disapproved of his actions. This helps explain Reuben's fearful statement and question when he found Joseph missing from the cistern—"'The boy isn't there! *Where can I turn now?*'"

Reuben's plan to rescue Joseph and to take him back to his father had backfired (37:22). Predictably, he was terribly fearful that Joseph had escaped and was already on his way home to relate to Jacob the horrible story of what had happened. Ironically, Joseph would not have known that Reuben had devised a plan to save his life. Consequently, Joseph's report would seriously implicate Reuben in what had happened, even though his oldest brother had saved his life by suggesting that he be thrown into the cistern! In fact, Joseph probably knew nothing of his brothers' original plan to kill him. This conclusion is based on the fact that Joseph's brothers had their intense discussion *before* Joseph had even arrived on the scene (37:22–23).

Understandably, Reuben was scared to death! He found himself in a catch-22! We can now understand why he accepted his brothers' solution so quickly. He had no choice—apart from total repentance. Even if he had redeemed Joseph from the Ishmaelites, what had happened would still get back to his father. He would have had a tough time explaining his alternate plan to save Joseph—both to Jacob and to his little brother.

Deep Sorrow and Self-Punishment

Happy to be rid of Joseph, his brothers followed through with their insidious plan. They "slaughtered a goat and dipped the robe in the blood," and then took it back to their father and said shrewdly, "'We found this. Examine it to see whether it is your son's robe'" (37:31–32).

Jacob recognized the robe immediately and drew the conclusion they hoped he would. "'It is my son's robe!'" Jacob cried. "'Some ferocious animal has devoured him. Joseph has surely been torn to pieces'" (37:33).

Jacob's deep feelings of sorrow were accentuated because of his love for his favorite son. He "tore his clothes, put on sackcloth and mourned for his son many days." Furthermore, *he refused to be comforted.* We read that all of his children and grandchildren attempted to ease his pain, but his response was pathetic. "'No,'" he said, "'in mourning will I go down to the grave to my son'" (37:34–35).

How much of Jacob's emotional suffering related to his own mistakes and the guilt he now felt regarding his decision to send Joseph to check up on his sons? In some respects, Jacob knew his sons well; in other respects, he did not know them at all. He understood their outward behavior, but he knew little of—or perhaps ignored—their inner feelings. If he had been in touch with the intensity of their hatred, he would not have set Joseph up for such a terrible ordeal.

Reality has a way of jolting us out of our selfish behavior, our subjective reactions, and naive rationalizations. What a price to pay for irresponsibility! However, the truth remains: we reap what we sow!

But there is another reality. Self-punishment is not the answer. It only makes matters worse. But more about that later.

"Meanwhile," we read, "the Midianites sold Joseph in Egypt to Potiphar, one of Pharaoh's officials, the captain of the guard" (37:36). However, this introduces us to another action-packed chapter in a very dramatic story. At this point, let's pause to reflect on the lessons that emerge from what we've just studied.

Becoming God's Man Today

Principles to Live By

Principle 1. It's important to be in touch with our children's feelings.

It's easy to be out of touch with our children's feelings, even though we think we may understand them. This was certainly true of Jacob. And it can happen to us, particularly in our culture—and especially to fathers. In fact, if it happened to Jacob in a primitive and rural culture, how much more so in our twentieth-century "rat-race" society.

The Absentee Father Syndrome

Many fathers in our Western culture are, of necessity, away from their children many hours a week—in some instances, all week. And when we come home from what is often a very grueling and emotionally demanding vocation, we are anything but in the mood to relate to our children—their problems, their needs, their concerns. And if our wives also work outside the home, both of us may avoid finding out about our children's problems so as to escape any emotional involvement. In fact, in this kind of environment, parents naturally want to spend time by themselves—not with their children—and the neglect is multiplied.

"I Really Didn't Know My Daughter Until . . ."

I discovered how easy it is to think you know your children, and then discover there is a lot you don't know, when one of my daughters was in the third grade. Because of a serious illness, she had to stay out of school for a number of weeks and got considerably behind in her studies. When she was finally able to return to school, her teacher gave me permission to take her to the public library one afternoon a week to assist her in her studies.

I was amazed at what I discovered about her during those times together—the questions she would never ask in school, her feelings about life, her questions about what she was studying, about Christianity, about her family, and about me. One question that troubled her deeply—even at eight years old—was why innocent people suffer! I must admit I really didn't begin to know my daughter until that time together. And I'm sure there are still many things I don't know. But it was a very enlightening start.

There is no substitute for quality time spent with our children. But it must be time that relates to their own interests and needs—which, of course, change as they grow older, and vary with individuals, and certainly vary between the sexes. And we must remember that "availability only" will not be enough. In other words, it doesn't work to simply say, "OK, I'm available! Talk to me!"

One of Our Greatest Investments

My first two children were girls. When they became young teens, I discovered there weren't too many things junior high girls have in common with their father. A social relationship with their peers is far more important to them emotionally than their social relationship with their father. That's just a reality!

When they were younger, I had taught them to water ski in a summer camping experience. They loved it! Consequently, I saw an opportunity to tap into something they enjoyed doing with their friends—but where they *needed me.* So, my wife and I agreed to purchase a ski boat. Though it took every bit of savings we had at the time, I'd do it all over again. During the summer, I would often spend an entire day at the lake driving the boat so they could ski, not so much with me, but with their friends!

Be a Good Listener!

You see, it wasn't really "Dad and his girls" spending time together. Rather, it was Dad providing an opportunity for his girls and their friends to be together. I spent a lot of time *just listening* to their conversations. What a learning experience!

And, of course, they really appreciated what I was doing—especially when their friends told them (when I wasn't listening) they thought my girls had a great dad!

I also discovered there are times when a father should sit and listen to other conversations—particularly at the dinner table. In fact, it's best sometimes to not ask questions, make comments, or offer suggestions—unless asked. And even then, you might be better off to say very little. It's amazing what you'll learn about your children's inner feelings when they are given uninterrupted time to just talk—without adult comments!

So, what can we learn from Jacob? We may think we know our children, when in reality we know very little about their inner thoughts and feelings. Somehow we must circumvent the demands of our culture and get to know them as they really are.

Principle 2. We must not allow self-protection to cause us to put our children on a performance standard.

Jacob demonstrated more concern over his own reputation than he did over the fact that his sons had been involved in sinful and evil practices. When Simeon and Levi committed murder, he stated, "'You have brought trouble on *me* by making *me* a stench to the . . . people living in this land'" (34:30).

How easy it is to fall into this same psychological and egotistical trap! As parents, we can become more concerned about our own image than the real problems facing our children. And when we put our children on a performance standard, it creates resentment.

As a pastor, I tried to learn this lesson early on in my relationship with my children. I'd seen so many spiritual leaders put their children on a performance standard, expecting certain behaviors to make themselves look good. Sadly, their children grew up resenting the "ministry"—and in some cases, the Lord Himself! All children want to be accepted and loved for who they are, not for what they do. I haven't always practiced this principle as I should have, but I've tried.

There is a balance here, of course. If we maintain that balance early in their lives—loving them unconditionally and reassuring them of our love when we have to discipline them—our children will grow up wanting to make us look good rather than bad.

Principle 3. Passive fathers (parents) can create insecurity and anger in their children.

Jacob might be classified as the proverbial "passive father." When his sons, Levi and Simeon, murdered the Shechemites, and when Reuben committed incest with Bilhah, he did little about it except harbor it in his heart and then lower the boom on all three sons just before he died.

This is another trait of passive persons. Rather than dealing with problems immediately, they carry grudges and later make the person pay for their sins. Avoid this approach with your children. Be actively involved in their lives—*now!* Give them correction—*now!* And more than anything, encourage them—*now!*

Principle 4. We reap what we sow, but self-punishment is not the answer to our problems.

Jacob refused to be comforted because of what had happened to Joseph. More than we probably know, this refusal was based on the fact that he knew that he had made some serious mistakes. He was determined to mourn—and punish himself—until he died.

Like Jacob, all of us make mistakes and sin against our children. Unfortunately, some of these errors in judgment create problems that are in some respects irreversible. But it does not help to go through life blaming ourselves. Furthermore, it is not God's will. There is forgiveness in Christ. We must accept that forgiveness. And if we have sinned against our children, we must *sincerely* seek their forgiveness. If our motives for confession are to reform them, they'll sense it. However, if our motive in seeking forgiveness is godly sorrow, they'll sense that too. And then if they refuse to forgive, we must move forward with our own lives demonstrating Christ's love in our future relationships.

It's very sad when parents go through life punishing themselves, and it's equally wrong for children to go through life blaming their parents for their problems. As children become adults and face life, they must recognize that they are responsible for their own actions—no matter what happened to them as children.

Personalizing These Principles

1. To what extent am I aware of my children's true feelings?

   A SUGGESTION: Look for opportunities to listen carefully to what they're saying, both in their words and actions.

   AN INSIGHT: Actions may often reveal the opposite of what the child is really feeling.

2. Am I putting my children on a performance standard?

   A SUGGESTION: Avoid telling your children not to embarrass you, either by direct statement or by implication.

   AN INSIGHT: Angry children will get angrier when this happens.

3. Am I too passive as a parent?

   A SUGGESTION: Ask your wife for her opinion. If you don't agree with her opinion, ask a friend who will be objective and honest.

   AN INSIGHT: "Being passive" and "learning to listen" are two different things.

4. Am I punishing myself for mistakes that I've made with my children?

A SUGGESTION: Sincerely seek forgiveness for mistakes. Honestly correct what you can, accept what you cannot change, and go on from that point doing the will of God.

AN INSIGHT: Even if you're sincere, your children may test you to reassure themselves that you are *really* sincere.

Set a Goal

First of all, be encouraged with the principles you *are* applying well. But then, ask yourself what principle have you violated the most. For example, you may have been giving your children the impression you're personally embarrassed by their behavior. Though these are normal emotions, what goal can you set that will enable you to assure your children you're more concerned about their feelings than about your own?

_____

_____

_____

_____

Memorize the Following Scripture

If we confess our sins, he is faithful and just and will forgive us our sins and purify us from all unrighteousness.

1 JOHN 1:9

Growing Together

The following questions are designed for small group discussion:

1. What principles do you feel you have applied well in the parenting process? If you're not a parent, what principles do you feel your father (and/or mother) applied well with you?

2. If you feel free to do so, share a principle you feel you're violating the most. If you're not a parent, what principle do you feel your father (and/or mother) violated the most?

3. What has been the greatest learning experience you've had as a parent-either positively or negatively? If not a parent, what is the greatest thing you've learned from your father (and/or mother)?

4. What would you do differently if you could do things all over again? What would you do the same?

5. What can we pray for you specifically?

Chapter 4

Overcoming Sexual Temptation
Read Genesis 39:1–20

*I*n view of what's happening to the values in our own society, this segment of Joseph's life is probably one of the most relevant to our lives today—particularly as men. Sadly, I've seen some of my closest friends give in to sexual temptation. In some cases, it has destroyed their entire families. It startles me every time it happens and makes me realize how weak most of us are in this area of our lives. It serves as a "wake up call"!

In this study, we'll see how Joseph handled intense sexual temptation and chose to follow God's will rather than to violate his moral codes. However, his choice cost him dearly. He went from having one of the highest and most respected servant roles in Egypt to being sentenced to years in prison. What is most encouraging, however, is that God never forsook Joseph. In fact, God used this experience to prepare him for an even greater position in the Egyptian kingdom.

The focus of this dramatic saga now moves directly to Joseph. We'll meet his family again, but not until a number of years have come and gone. God's providential spotlight will remain on Joseph for the next major era of his life.

Apart from his prophetic dreams, Joseph had no clue as to what was happening to him. However, after years of painful suffering, he would discover that God had a special place for him in the unique and turbulent history of His chosen people. But Joseph could not occupy that place until he was adequately prepared—both spiritually and emotionally. Though the Lord was preparing him during his younger years, his intensive preparation began in Egypt.

Potiphar's Purchase

When the Midianite merchants arrived in Egypt, they sold Joseph to Potiphar, a high-ranking Egyptian official who is identified in Scripture as "captain of the guard" (39:1). In other words, Potiphar was the lead man in Pharaoh's team of bodyguards, which also means the king of Egypt placed his total trust in this man.

But we also know from other sources he was "chief of the executioners." This was an even more awesome position. It was Potiphar's responsibility to implement the death penalty for criminal behavior. He was indeed a prominent man in Egypt.

God's Protection

Joseph's brothers may have forgotten about their brother they had so cruelly sold into slavery, but not Joseph's God! "The LORD *was with Joseph and he prospered*" (39:2). We read that *"the Lord gave him success in everything he did"* (39:3).

We're not told anything about Joseph's first duties. We can assume he was assigned the most menial tasks under constant supervision and surveillance. But Joseph's character and faithfulness eventually became obvious to Potiphar. What he did, insignificant as it may have been, he did well. He was cooperative, not rebellious. Though he may have been pampered and even spoiled by his father, he was an intelligent and motivated young man who quickly perceived that he was in a set of circumstances beyond his direct control and he decided to make the best of it. And at some point in time he was assigned to live and serve in Potiphar's home (39:2).

What happened to Joseph is a graphic and powerful illustration of what Jesus taught His disciples hundreds of years later—a servant who has "been faithful with a few things" will be put "in charge of many things" (Matt. 25:21). This is exactly what happened to this young slave. Joseph fully used what he had at his disposal, and God honored his efforts.

This high-ranking official recognized that Joseph was no ordinary man. In fact, Joseph had such an outstanding testimony that Potiphar, who worshiped the "gods" of Egypt, came to understand that Joseph served a very special God. More specifically, Potiphar concluded "that the LORD was with him and that the LORD gave him success in everything he did" (39:3). How wonderful it would be if every Christian living today had this kind of vibrant witness for the Lord Jesus Christ!

"The LORD Was with Him"

We really don't know what this statement means in every detail (39:3). However, we can speculate on the basis of some well-known facts. Potiphar certainly did not know and believe in the living God who was worshiped by Abraham, Isaac, and Jacob. Rather, he was a ruthless, pagan man who was an idolater. But in some way, he recognized that Joseph's abilities and success were more than natural; they were supernatural!

Daniel's Predecessor

Perhaps Potiphar saw Joseph kneel and pray to God, just as Daniel did years later when he was in Babylonian captivity. Like Joseph, Daniel was a very successful man in all he did in government circles. One of his secrets was to ask God for help. "Three times a day he got down on his knees and prayed" (Dan. 6:10). He did not hide the fact that he worshiped God. In fact, his prayer times were so obvious and successful, other government officials were threatened and jealous, which eventually landed him in a den of lions.

This is a convicting point. How many Christians today hesitate to bow their heads and pray in public? If we're honest, we'd have to admit that we're intimidated—or even ashamed. Yet this can become a powerful way to demonstrate our faith in the one true God!

Jacob's Model

Though we've noted Jacob's weaknesses in previous chapters, he also had some great spiritual strengths. We must not forget that. This was especially true in his later years after he "saw God face to face" on his return trip to Canaan (Gen. 32:22–32). At this point in time, the Lord even changed his name to Israel. This is very significant, for the name *Jacob* meant "trickster" or "deceiver," and his new name, *Israel,* meant "to persist with God."

After Jacob's personal encounter with the Lord, Joseph must have seen his father often offer up sacrifices and prayers. When God instructed Jacob to leave Shechem and to build an altar in Bethel—the place he had first met God years before—he not only obeyed but he instructed everyone in his household, including his servants and everyone associated with him, to "get rid of the foreign gods" they had brought with them on their trip back from Canaan (35:1–5).

Though not perfect in his judgments as a father, from this point forward, Jacob was a different man. Even his change of name reflected his new perspective on spiritual values. Naturally, this would impact young Joseph who was very close to his father.

Potiphar saw these spiritual values reflected in Joseph's attitudes and actions. He understood that there was a direct cause-effect relationship between Joseph's devotion to God and his successful career as a servant in his household. Consequently, Potiphar eventually promoted Joseph to be "in charge of his household" (39:4).

The Ultimate in Trust

Joseph's behavior was so outstanding and above reproach that he became Potiphar's executive assistant. This man of power and wealth entrusted to his care "everything he owned" (39:4). This meant supervising all the other servants and employees, handling Potiphar's public relations, overseeing his finances, administering his agricultural interests and all of his other business activities. In fact, Potiphar "did not concern himself with anything except the food he ate" (39:6).

How could this happen? It seems impossible. From a human point of view, it was. At this point, we must remember the words of the angel Gabriel to the virgin Mary when he proclaimed, "'For nothing is impossible with God'" (Luke 1:37).

Though Joseph's credibility was certainly related to his personal performance, there was a more basic and deciding factor in Potiphar's mind. Not only did Joseph prosper in all that he did, but *"the LORD blessed the household of the Egyptian because of Joseph."* In fact, *"the blessing of the LORD was on everything Potiphar had, both in the house and in the field"* (39:5).

Never before had this man ever seen his people so motivated and his crops so productive. It's no wonder Potiphar trusted Joseph and promoted him to such a high position. Potiphar believed he couldn't lose. It really didn't matter to him which "god" was causing all this success as long as it continued. His pagan theological system certainly could absorb Joseph's religious point of view—particularly when it involved material success. Money talks, and Potiphar recognized in Joseph an incredible discovery.

Potiphar's Wife

Potiphar was not the only one who was taken with Joseph. Eventually, Potiphar's wife "took notice" of him as well (39:6–10). However, her motives were quite different from her husband's.

Potiphar's wife was anything but subtle. Her proposition to Joseph was straightforward and direct. "'Come to bed with me!'" she said (39:7).

It's possible, of course, that this woman's sexual interest in Joseph may have been motivated by a number of other factors. Perhaps it was jealousy because of her husband's esteem for Joseph. Or, maybe Potiphar was too busy doing other things rather than meeting her emotional and physical needs.

It's also possible that her motives were based on revenge. In view of the moral value system in the Egyptian culture, Potiphar probably had other women in his life.

Remember, too, that women in Egypt at this time were more liberated than any other place in the world. The biblical text, however, gives us the most obvious reason as to why Potiphar's wife was attracted to Joseph. We simply read that "Joseph was well-built and handsome" (39:6). He was appealing to her—and a real challenge. Perhaps this is all the explanation we need.

Remarkable Resistance

Potiphar's wife was, in many respects, Joseph's superior. He was her servant. Also, Joseph was surrounded by negative examples. Immorality permeated the Egyptian culture. Joseph's brothers had not been paragons of virtue either. In view of the environment, his resistance is remarkable!

Joseph's resistance to temptation is even more remarkable in view of this woman's persistence. Not only was her invitation direct, but she kept after him *"day after day"* (39:10). And we need not even speculate to conclude that her invitation was more than verbal. She would have used every visual seductive technique she could think of. But "day after day" Joseph "refused to go to bed with her or even be with her" (39:10).

Remember, too, that Joseph's own knowledge of God's laws was limited. Many, many years prior, God's thundering voice came from Sinai when He said to the children of Israel,

"'You shall not commit adultery. You shall not covet your neighbor's wife'" (Exod. 20:14, 17). It would be another four hundred years before the Lord led His people out of Egypt back to Canaan. But in spite of Joseph's limited knowledge of God's laws, in spite of the bad examples both in his family and in Egypt, in spite of his own natural desires and tendencies, and—perhaps most significant—in spite of the natural opportunity to cooperate in a relatively safe, secret setting, Joseph still resisted!

Reasons for Resistance

There are at least three reasons why Joseph continually resisted this sexual temptation.

Potiphar's Trust

Joseph would not violate Potiphar's trust. "'No one is greater in this house than I am,'" he told her. *"My master has withheld nothing from me except you, because you are his wife"* (39:9).

Joseph knew Potiphar trusted him totally—even with his wife. Otherwise, why would this powerful man leave Joseph completely in charge, knowing he would not take advantage of his wife's sexual overtures—behavior he probably knew would happen? Potiphar would have to be totally naive not to know about his wife's potential interest in Joseph. This makes the responsibility he gave Joseph and the trust he put in him even more amazing.

Spiritual Values

More importantly, Joseph would not violate his spiritual convictions. He would not disobey God. Though he was limited in his knowledge of God's laws, he knew the Lord personally and he believed in his heart that it would be wrong to engage in sexual relations with Potiphar's wife or any woman who was not his own wife. He had strong moral convictions; he would not allow himself to *"sin against God"* (39:9).

God's Reputation

Joseph resisted this temptation for another reason. Though more subtle in the biblical record, it's still obvious. Joseph did not want to hurt God's reputation.

Let's not forget that Potiphar was well aware of Joseph's faith in God. He had observed this young man's ethical and moral convictions that were based on his relationship with God. This is why Potiphar trusted him so completely. For Joseph to violate the Lord's will in this matter would certainly interfere with whatever interest Potiphar had in the one, true God. It would destroy his witness. Potiphar's interest in the God of Abraham, Isaac, and Jacob went beyond what he observed in Joseph's life. He also knew that he was being blessed because of Joseph's God. For Joseph to violate Potiphar's trust in him would undermine any trust his master was developing in the God who made Joseph trustworthy.

Falsely Accused

To resist temptation and be rewarded is one thing. To resist and get into serious trouble is yet another. From a human perspective, Joseph paid a terrible price for his faithful stand (39:11–20).

On one occasion Joseph entered the house to care for his responsibilities, and once again he encountered Potiphar's wife—alone! Not a single servant was in the house, a definite setup. She was trying to remove every reason for Joseph to resist her advances.

Being more aggressive than ever, she grabbed his cloak and pulled him in her direction. Joseph instantly resisted, pulling in the opposite direction. Her grip was firm, for he left her standing alone with his cloak in her hand as he literally "ran out of the house" (39:12).

Prior to this aggressive approach, Joseph resisted graciously. After all, he was her servant. This time there was no way he could resist graciously. Joseph's actions were overt and sudden. And so was her response. Intense sexual advances combined with overt rejection often generate some intense hostility. This is exactly what happened. Her cries of rage could be heard throughout the house.

Quickly and impulsively, Potiphar's wife twisted the story. Her lust turned to hatred. Screaming for her servants, she accused Joseph of attempted rape, and when Potiphar came home, she repeated her twisted story, showing him Joseph's cloak to prove her point. The Scriptures state that Potiphar "burned with anger" and he immediately had Joseph imprisoned (39:19–20).

Under ordinary circumstances, a man accused of such actions in the Egyptian culture would have been put to death. But how much more so when it involved the wife of Potiphar who was "chief of the executioners." A simple word would have meant Joseph's head—immediately!

Why did Potiphar have mercy on Joseph? Certainly God's hand of protection was upon Joseph, for God had a unique plan for his life. But, from a human perspective, Potiphar probably suspected his wife was lying. Perhaps his anger was directed more at her than at Joseph. After all, to save face he would now have to take action against the man who had brought him so much success. Considering his own prominent position in Egypt, he had no choice. He had to do something. He chose to allow Joseph to live—but in prison.

Becoming God's Man Today

Principles to Live By

Principle 1. When we are the most successful, we are often the most vulnerable to sexual temptation.

How true in Joseph's case! His success was even caused by God's blessing, but it did not insulate him from Satan.

No matter what our success, we must be on guard in a particular way, for this is often when the enemy will strike. If Satan can catch us with our guard down, he may at that moment deliver a devastating blow. Before we know what has happened, we may find ourselves in a compromising situation, particularly if we yield in some way.

The apostle Paul stated it very directly to the Corinthians: "So, if you think you are standing firm, be careful that you don't fall!" (1 Cor. 10:12).

Principle 2. To resist temptation, we must have firm moral and ethical convictions based on a biblical value system.

Again, Joseph beautifully illustrates this principle. He was determined he would not violate the trust placed in him by Potiphar nor would he "sin against God."

Human Accountability

The order here is very important. It moves from the human to the divine. There are people who trust us not to yield to temptation—our children, our marital partners, our fellow Christians, and last but not least, many of our non-Christian friends and associates. Having firm convictions and desires not to violate their trust is a great source of strength. This is why having an accountability partner is so important.

Divine Accountability

The most important motivating source for not yielding to temptation should be our relationship with God. Furthermore, the strongest deterrent ought to focus in His love and grace toward us—not our fear of what He might do or allow to happen to us if we sin. Certainly fear of God's discipline should be a factor, but our primary motivation should be that stated by Paul to Titus: "For the grace of God that brings salvation has appeared to all men. It teaches us to say 'No' to ungodliness and worldly passions, and to live self-controlled, upright and godly lives in this present age, while we wait for the blessed hope—the glorious appearing of our great God and Savior, Jesus Christ, who gave himself for us to redeem us from all wickedness and to purify for himself a people that are his very own, eager to do what is good" (Titus 2:11–14).

Principle 3. To resist temptation, we must avoid verbal and visual stimuli.

There is a phrase in Joseph's story that is easy to miss and yet it is a key in overcoming temptation. Not only did Joseph consistently refuse the invitation from Potiphar's wife, but he eventually refused to *"even be with her"* (39:10).

There are many temptations that are generated by verbal and visual stimuli. We can never avoid them all. To do so we would have to leave this world. But we do have certain controls over our environment. For example, what we subject ourselves to, particularly in the world of entertainment, does affect our thoughts, our desires, and our behavior. When what we hear and see on a regular basis promote values that are out of harmony with God's will, we are setting ourselves up for a fall; when we play with fire, we'll eventually get painfully burned!

Much of what is happening today is flagrant. We can recognize it and avoid it. But we must also avoid subtle messages. Several years ago, my wife and teenage son were watching a TV movie entitled "The Kid from Nowhere" featuring Beau Bridges and Susan St. James and a retarded boy they called Johnnie. Susan played the part of a mother who gave birth to the retarded child and subsequently was deserted by her husband because he couldn't handle the problem. However, she hung in there admirably and became very devoted to the child in spite of the many difficulties she faced.

Beau played the part of a coach in a school for retarded and disabled children. He took a keen interest in Johnnie and wanted to involve him in the sports program. His mother was desperately fearful that her son might get injured. Eventually, the coach convinced the mother she should allow Johnnie to participate, which helped him greatly; it even helped him to win a very coveted award in a Special Olympics program designed for challenged children. He showed tremendous compassion for the boy, as only Beau Bridges can exude in movie parts like this one.

But there was more to the story. He fell in love with the boy's mother. Eventually, after a great deal of persistence on his part, they got together for an evening over dinner at her home. After the meal, the coach tucked the boy into bed—a very loving and tender scene—and then proceeded to communicate his love to the boy's mother. She began to respond. Though she did not allow the relationship to culminate that night because of the emotional pain in her past, it was obvious that the value system portrayed was that if their love was real, it would, under normal circumstances, culminate in sexual intercourse.

It was not a sensuous scene. Rather, it was far more powerful. All along, the coach and the mother had demonstrated spiritual values reflecting compassion and concern for Johnnie and other forgotten children in a way that would put many Christians to shame—including yours truly. And in the midst of that beautiful mood and powerful setting, they presented a scene that communicated if you're really in love, sexual intercouse is what should happen. By this time, we—the audience—would be so moved by the overall value system in the film, we would have a difficult time accepting the fact that their overall intent was wrong, even if God said it was wrong!

That is subtle—and powerful! And the most subtle part of all was when the coach, recognizing her resistance and why, said, "I'm sorry. I've moved too quickly. Can I just stay, lie beside you, and just hold you the rest of the night?" This was the finishing touch! In some respects, there was more true love in that statement than in any other, but the overall context involved motivations that were a violation of the will of God.

Let us beware! Satan is subtle. I'm not suggesting we should avoid all TV movies. This was a good one—one of the best! But we'd better discern the subtle messages. They're sometimes more powerful than flagrant violence and sex.

*Principle 4. Some people yield to sexual temptation,
not because of uncontrollable lust, but because of a fear
of rejection and a loss of position.*

Joseph's temptation was sexual. But it was more. He would naturally fear rejection and loss of position. He had to know in his heart that he was in danger of losing everything he had gained. He is a classic example of a person who is "caught between a rock and a hard place." He was in a no-win situation.

A single temptation may have several facets—touching other areas of our lives. Furthermore, there are also many kinds of temptations. One of the most common in our culture—and in every culture since sin entered into the world—is the kind illustrated in Joseph's experience. Sexual desire is normal and often causes people to violate God's will, leading to many heartaches.

But temptation also focuses on material things, which may be legitimate in themselves. Furthermore, a temptation for material things can also be intricately related with sexual temptation.

The apostle John summarized it most clearly when he wrote, "Do not love the world or anything in the world. If anyone loves the world, the love of the Father is not in him. For everything in the world—the cravings of sinful man, the lust of his eyes and the boasting of what he has and does—comes not from the Father but from the world. The world and its desires pass away, but the man who does the will of God lives forever" (1 John 2:15–17).

*Principle 5. When we resist temptation, we may pay a
price with people, but ultimately never with God.*

Joseph *did* pay a price—a painful price. But eventually God honored him for his righteous stand. And God will do the same for us. People may reject us, scoff at us, and even tell lies about us, trying to make us look bad. But God will never forget!

We must remember, also, that Joseph's experience was both a temptation and a trial. This is difficult to comprehend, for

God does not tempt—Satan does (Jas. 1:13). But God does allow trials—often that we might grow spiritually (1 Pet. 1:7). He is often preparing us for greater responsibility in His kingdom. And to complicate matters in our own minds, God can actually take evil (which is caused by Satan) and can make it work for good (Rom. 8:28). Eventually Joseph would learn this in his future experience.

God can turn "lemons" into "lemonade" if we'll let Him. All is not lost, even if we stumble and fall. There is forgiveness in Jesus Christ. We can begin anew. There are things in the past we cannot change, but with His help, we can make significant changes in the future—and be at peace within ourselves.

Personalizing These Principles

Following are some questions to help you apply in your own life the principles we've learned from Joseph.

1. Am I aware that we are more prone to sexual temptation when we are the most successful—spiritually, domestically, vocationally, and socially?

2. Do I have firm convictions that are based squarely on God's Word which will enable me to withstand sexual temptations? Have I made myself accountable to another Christian—or group of Christians?

3. Do I avoid verbal and visual stimuli that weaken my resistance to sexual temptation?

4. Do I realize that sexual temptation is often related to a fear of rejection or loss of position or even a desire for material things?

5. Do I truly believe that God will honor my refusal to become involved in sinful attitudes and actions?

Set a Goal

Review the Principles to Live By in this chapter and select the one that relates most specifically to your own present situation. For example, you may have difficulty controlling what you watch in the media. Write out a specific goal to help you apply the principle you choose for your life:

_____

_____

_____

_____

Memorize the Following Scripture

No temptation has seized you except what is common to man. And God is faithful; he will not let you be tempted beyond what you can bear. But when you are tempted, he will also provide a way out so that you can stand up under it.
1 CORINTHIANS 10:13

Growing Together

The following questions are designed for small group discussion:

1. Why are men often vulnerable to sexual temptation when they are most successful?

2. What other factors cause men to be vulnerable sexually?

3. Would you feel free to share when you are the most vulnerable to sexual temptation?

4. How do you avoid succumbing to sexual temptation?

5. What can we pray for you specifically?

Chapter 5

God's Presence in Prison
Read Genesis 39:20–23; 40:1–23

I've never experienced the pain of being falsely accused and sent to prison—and I hope I never will! But as I reflected on Joseph's experience, my mind went back to a time in my own life when I was falsely accused and terribly humiliated by several men who I thought were my friends. They totally violated my trust and at the same time sowed seeds of doubts about my character in the hearts of many people—some who were my closest friends. Eventually, God vindicated me and everyone knew the truth.

While these men were falsely accusing me, they were involved in some very sinful behavior themselves. I later discovered that one of their reasons for attacking me was that I was getting too close to uncovering their secrets. Unfortunately, this kind of "smoke screen" behavior has been around for a long time, but this was the first time I had experienced it.

Needless to say, it was terribly painful. Nothing hurts as much as when those you've trusted, believed in, and provided unique opportunities for advancement tell outright lies and strategize to destroy you without regard for your own sense of well-being and the feelings of your family.

God Set the Record Straight

God eventually vindicated me in ways I could never have defended myself. But before He did, I often struggled with attitudes and feelings that were difficult to control. By seeking God's help, however, I was able to forgive these men before I ever knew the true reasons for their actions. Though I certainly struggled with bouts of anger and depression during that time, God gave me the strength to not allow a root of bitterness to creep into my soul.

In this situation, I decided to allow God to be my defender— though it is not wrong to defend yourself when you're falsely accused. Paul certainly illustrates this in his own life. But in this instance, my closest confidants counseled me to allow God to handle the situation. It was good advice. Eventually He did just that—in a way that revealed the truth to everyone. Though I had to wait patiently over a lengthy period of time, it happened. When God took action, there were no "ifs," "ands," or "buts" about the truth.

Will It Never End?

Joseph stands out in the Old Testament as a classic example of one who was repeatedly mistreated. During the first thirty years of his life, he probably experienced more injustice than any biblical character other than Jesus Christ.[1] He was scorned and rejected by his brothers when he was sincerely seeking to find out how they were doing. Because of their jealousy and hatred, he was physically abused and sold as a slave into Egypt. When tempted by Potiphar's wife, he refused to yield and was falsely accused of sexual harassment. He was then unjustly removed from his high-ranking position in Potiphar's house and put in prison. And in this chapter, we'll see that, while imprisoned, he was forgotten by the man he had helped and encouraged the most.

Joseph knew firsthand what mistreatment really was. I'm sure he thought it would never end. Though he must have had bouts with anger and depression, he did not allow bitterness or self-pity to wither his soul. Joseph is a marvelous example of Christlike behavior in the Old Testament.

God's Repeat Performance

The next installment in Joseph's life story sounds repetitious. And it is—by divine design! Notice the following similarities:

JOSEPH IN POTIPHAR'S HOUSE	JOSEPH IN PRISON
God's Presence	
"The LORD was with Joseph" (39:2).	"But while Joseph was there in the prison, *the LORD was with him"* (39:20–21).
Trustworthy	
"Joseph found *favor in his eyes* and became his attendant" (39:4).	"The LORD . . . granted him *favor in the eyes* of the prison warden" (39:21).
Responsibility	
"Potiphar *put him in charge* of his household, and he entrusted to his care *everything he owned"* (39:4).	"The warden *put Joseph in charge* of all those held in prison, and he was made responsible for *all that was done there"* (39:22).
Delegation	
"With Joseph in charge, *he did not concern himself with anything* except the food he ate" (39:6).	"The warden *paid no attention to anything* under Joseph's care" (39:23).
Success	
Potiphar trusted Joseph because he saw "that *the LORD gave him success in everything he did"* (39:3).	The prison warden trusted Joseph because he, too, saw that *"the LORD . . . gave him success in whatever he did"* (39:23).

Powerful Parallels

The parallels in these two experiences are very clear.

God's Continual Presence

When Joseph was scorned by his brothers and sold into Egyptian slavery, God did not forsake him. And when he was sent to prison by Potiphar, again, the Lord stayed by his side. God never forgot Joseph, nor did He leave him.

A Trustworthy Man

When Joseph began his duties as Potiphar's slave, he demonstrated positive attitudes and "found favor in his eyes." Just so, God also granted Joseph "favor in the eyes of the prison warden." He was noticed by both men. He was both a model slave and a model prisoner.

Unusual Responsibility

Because of Joseph's faithfulness combined with God's presence, this young man was promoted and given a high-level supervisory task, first in Potiphar's household and then in prison. In both situations, he was given overall and complete responsibility.

Incredible Delegation

The fourth similarity demonstrates the results of trust. Both Potiphar and the warden turned everything over to Joseph and did not worry about a thing. It appears they came to the point in their ability to trust Joseph that they did not even check up on him. They delegated everything to him and put him totally in charge. They knew he would not let them down.

Consistent Success

The fifth parallel is the most important. It indicates why these men trusted Joseph so completely. Both men saw a very definite correlation between the God Joseph worshiped and the success he enjoyed. Neither Potiphar nor the prison warden missed seeing this divine connection. The "God factor" was highly visible. Both men were greatly impressed.

Shackles and Irons

Though Joseph was eventually given a great deal of freedom along with responsibility to manage the prison, his initial time was very difficult. The psalmist tells us that "they bruised his feet with shackles" and "his neck was put in irons" (Ps. 105:18). We're not told how long he experienced this kind of bondage. But we do know that it was long enough for the shackles to cause serious bruises and wounds. And we also know that Joseph's attitudes and actions throughout the whole ordeal were incredibly exemplary for one who had been so mistreated by his own family and was now innocently incarcerated by the man whose trust he refused to violate.

The Cupbearer and Baker

Eventually, Joseph was rewarded with a degree of freedom and unusual responsibility within the prison itself. One day he was assigned two men who were not the average, run-of-the-mill prisoners. They were the "cupbearer and the baker of the king of Egypt" (Gen. 40:1)—representing two very responsible positions.

The cupbearer was a man who was so highly trusted that he tasted the king's food and drink to make sure no one would attempt to poison him. Furthermore, the king usually took his cupbearer into his confidence, seeking his advice on very important matters. Many years later, Nehemiah fulfilled this responsibility for King Artaxerxes (Neh. 1:11; 2:1).

The baker likewise was a very trusted man. He supervised all food preparation. If anyone was going to try to assassinate the king, it would probably begin in the king's kitchen. In this sense, the cupbearer and the baker worked closely together to protect their sovereign. If someone did slip poison into the king's food and drink, the cupbearer unfortunately would be the first to discover it—probably before it was too late to save his own life. He was very dependent, then, on the baker to keep it from happening in the first place.

We're not told why these men were sentenced to prison, except that they "offended their master, the king of Egypt" (Gen. 40:1). However, from the overall story, we can conjecture that the baker was probably more guilty than the cupbearer. In fact, it may be that, since these men worked so closely together, the cupbearer was guilty only by association. But whatever the crime, it was no doubt very serious. They were not just dismissed; they were put in prison!

Not only were the cupbearer and the baker confined to the same prison as Joseph, but they were also assigned to Joseph by "the captain of the guard" (40:4)—who was evidently none other than Potiphar, the man responsible for Joseph's own incarceration (39:1). If this observation is accurate, it adds credence to the hypothesis that Potiphar knew in his heart that Joseph had never been guilty of trying to rape his wife. Personally, I believe Potiphar may have had an important part in building a bridge between Joseph and the prison warden. Could this be why there are so many similarities between the way both of these men treated Joseph? Remember that God frequently blends human and divine factors in accomplishing His purposes in this world.

Note also that Joseph "attended" these men. They were not ordinary prisoners. Because of their high-level positions in the king's court, Potiphar must have given them special privileges and treatment. He assigned them to Joseph since he knew they would get special care!

Two Dreams

After the cupbearer and the baker "had been in custody for some time," both men had dreams—on the same night (40:4–19). The content of each dream was so uniquely related to each man's vocation and so similar in other respects that they instinctively must have known their dreams were not just a bizarre manifestation of their subconscious anxiety and fear. Consequently, they were even more afraid. When "Joseph came to them the next morning," he couldn't help but notice their dejection (40:6). "'Why are your faces so sad today?'" he asked (40:7).

They told Joseph what had happened, but made it clear that they didn't understand the meaning of these dreams. Joseph's response reflects his own growing relationship with God in the midst of difficulties as well as his boldness in letting others know what he believed. "'Do not interpretations belong to God?'" he asked. "'Tell me your dreams'" (40:8). This final statement by Joseph let them know—and anyone else who might be listening—that he believed that God would help him explain the meaning of their dreams.

Restoration for the Cupbearer

The cupbearer shared first. He saw a vine with three branches that very quickly produced grapes. He then saw himself squeezing the juice into Pharaoh's cup and serving him (40:9–11).

Interpreting the dream, Joseph told the cupbearer that in three days he would be restored to his position. But Joseph then added a personal request. "'But when all goes well with you, remember me and show me kindness; mention me to Pharaoh and get me out of this prison'" (40:14).

Joseph went on to relate to the cupbearer why he was in prison. "'I was forcibly carried off from the land of the Hebrews, and even here I have done nothing to deserve being put in a dungeon'" (40:15).

Joseph knew he was innocent and that this was God's divine moment for him to explain his predicament and ask for help. And I'm glad he did, for it indicates there's a time to defend ourselves against false accusations—even though God is the ultimate vindicator. There's also a time to ask someone to put in a good word for us even though we are trusting God with all our hearts to help us and to defend us.

Remember, however, that timing is very important. Had Joseph attempted to vindicate himself solely in his own efforts rather than waiting for God's moment in his life, he may never have gotten the unique opportunity that came his way that day. Wrong timing often causes legitimate self-defense to appear defensive.

Execution for the Chief Baker

The chief baker was watching and listening intently. It appears he had been hesitant to share his dream for fear the interpretation may not be favorable to his future welfare. And understandably so! Though certain elements in the two dreams were similar, some were different. And the chief baker was smart enough to know that his dream might be pointing to some serious consequences.

Nevertheless, he drew courage from Joseph's positive response to the cupbearer's dream and he related his own. In his dream, he was carrying three baskets of food containing "all kinds of baked goods for Pharaoh." However, as he walked along, carrying the baskets on his head, the birds swooped down and ate out of the baskets (40:16–17).

Joseph's response was just as quick as before and just as succinct. However, what he said was bad news—just as the baker had feared. "'The three baskets are three days,'" Joseph said—which was the similarity with the cupbearer's dream. Unfortunately for the baker, there was a dissimilarity. "'Within three days,'" Joseph stated, "'Pharaoh will lift off your head and hang you on a tree. And the birds will eat away your flesh'" (40:18–19). Hearing these words, the baker must have become paralyzed with fear!

Prophetic Realities

In three days, everything happened just as Joseph said it would (40:20–23). Pharaoh restored his cupbearer to his previous position but he had the chief baker executed. This may indicate that the chief baker was responsible for what had happened to get them imprisoned in the first place. That Pharaoh restored the cupbearer to such a prominent position demanding such total trust also points to this man's innocence. If he had been guilty of any serious wrong behavior, the king certainly would not have given his cupbearer another opportunity to protect him from assassination.

But the ironic part of the story is that once restored, the cupbearer did not remember Joseph who was in prison in spite of his innocence. Even though Joseph had taken personal interest in him when he was dejected and sad, the cupbearer did nothing about Joseph's personal request. He simply forgot.

We're not told why he forgot about Joseph. Was it just a bad memory? I don't think so! He may have been afraid to speak to Pharaoh about it for fear he would open some old wounds. Consequently, he may have just decided to forget. Or perhaps he was so enamored with his own restoration that he couldn't think about helping anybody else.

Whatever the reason, we simply read that he "did not remember Joseph; he forgot him" (40:23). After patiently waiting for a number of years for this kind of opportunity, Joseph was once again unjustly treated. But unknown to him, another opportunity was coming—an opportunity that was far greater than the one that passed him by. It would be another two years—but it was coming, and when it did it would be worth waiting for.

Becoming God's Man Today

Principles to Live By

For most of us, someone at some point in our lives has done something to us that we feel has been unfair and unjust. It may have involved a family member, a teacher, a friend, or an employer. It may have happened at home, at church, in school, or on the job. It may have taken place many years ago when we were children, or it may have been just yesterday. It may have happened once or many times. It may have involved harsh words, rejection, a rumor, physical abuse, false accusations, or unjust criticism. Or it may have been as simple as being taken for granted or being used for selfish purposes. And it may have been malicious or inadvertent. In some instances, it may have been our own perception of the situation. But whatever the experience, it was painful.

What can we learn from Joseph's example and how he handled injustice? For most of us, of course, his mistreatment makes anything we have experienced seem insignificant. On the other hand, any kind of injustice is emotionally painful and affects our behavior—both in the midst of the difficulties as well as when it is over. Joseph is a powerful example in both situations.

Principle 1. We must not allow bitterness to capture our souls.

Humanly speaking, Joseph had every reason to develop a bitter spirit. There had to be moments in his life when he was angry. After all, he was human. But there's a difference between getting angry and letting "the sun go down" while we're still angry. As Paul stated further in his letter to the Ephesians, this is what gives "the devil a foothold" in our lives (Eph. 4:26–27). Anger that is not dealt with will lead to lingering bitterness and all the other kinds of sinful behavior that result. And in the end, we not only hurt others but we also hurt ourselves. Bitterness and an unforgiving spirit is intensely self-destructive—emotionally, physically, and spiritually.

Don't misunderstand! This does not mean we cannot speak out against injustice even when that injustice is directed toward ourselves. Joseph did. He very clearly explained to the cupbearer that he had been mistreated and didn't belong in Egypt, let alone in an Egyptian prison. But he waited for God's timing, which is always a unique opportunity to defend ourselves without being or appearing defensive.

Why was Joseph able to handle this incredible and persistent mistreatment so well? This leads us to the next principle from his life.

Principle 2. We must not allow ourselves to turn against God; rather we must turn to God even more.

Many people who are mistreated allow their bitterness toward those who caused it to also be directed toward God. They blame the Lord for allowing it to happen.

Think about Joseph for a moment. Though he was not perfect and certainly was naive in his relationship with his brothers, in his heart he was reaching out to help them. Furthermore, he was only doing what his father had asked him to do. And in Egypt, he resisted temptation so as not to violate God's will or Potiphar's trust in him. And yet he was terribly mistreated for doing what was right.

Growing in Faith

Do you think Joseph was ever tempted to blame God? I'm confident he was. But he did not allow that temptation to result in sinful attitudes and actions. Rather, he grew in his relationship with God. Joseph trusted the Lord to be with him and to help him endure these crises.

In this sense, Joseph was projecting ahead many years in his difficult experience, and fleshing out the powerful truth stated by the apostle Peter, who, writing to Christian slaves in the first-century church, exhorted:

> Submit yourselves to your masters with all respect, not only to those who are good and considerate, but also to those who are harsh. For it is commendable if a man bears up under the pain of unjust suffering because he is conscious of God. But how is it to your credit if you receive a beating for doing wrong and endure it? But if you suffer for doing good and you endure it, this is commendable before God. To this you were called, because Christ suffered for you, leaving you an example, that you should follow in his steps. (1 Pet. 2:18–21)

Compounding the Problem

Fortunately, most of us have not had to face this kind of mistreatment. But how do we respond to the mistreatment we do face? No matter what the emotional or physical pain, we must not allow ourselves to become bitter toward God; for if we do, we will only compound our problem. Not that God will turn against us. He never will. His love is unconditional. The problem is that we have turned against Him, and in that state of mind we are violating all the necessary steps we must take to draw on Him as our divine Source of strength and help.

Principle 3. In some situations, particularly those beyond our control, we must patiently wait for God to vindicate us and to honor both our faith and our positive attitudes.

This must have been the most difficult thing Joseph had to do. His eleven years in Egypt was a long time, and most of that time was spent in prison. Following the request he made to the cupbearer, we're told that another *two years went by* before the cupbearer remembered what Joseph had done for him.

Once again, he had to wait patiently for God to set the record straight. The greatest temptation we all face when someone mistreats us is to seek revenge. Joseph certainly faced that temptation as well, but he overcame it. And in doing so, Joseph was not "overcome by evil." Rather he overcame "evil with good" (Rom. 12:21).

A Modern-Day Joseph

Is it possible to approach this kind of problem as Joseph did—to have the same attitudes? More than any other person, Corrie ten Boom stands out as a modern-day Joseph. She and her sister, Betsie, were placed in a Nazi concentration camp for hiding Jews in their home during World War II. While being terribly mistreated, Betsie died. Corrie's overall reaction to her predicament illustrates more powerfully Joseph's responses than anyone I know outside of Jesus Christ Himself. But she was human and she struggled desperately with forgiveness. One of Corrie's greatest tests came some time after she had been released. Listen to her own words as she describes this event:

> It was in a church in Munich that I saw him—a balding, heavy-set man in a gray overcoat, a brown felt hat clutched between

his hands. People were filing out of the basement room where I had just spoken, moving along the rows of wooden chairs to the door at the rear. It was 1947 and I had come from Holland to defeated Germany with the message that God forgives.

It was the truth they needed most to hear in that bitter, bombed-out land, and I gave them my favorite mental picture. Maybe because the sea is never far from a Hollander's mind, I liked to think that's where forgiven sins were thrown. "When we confess our sins," I said, "God casts them into the deepest ocean, gone forever. And even though I cannot find a Scripture for it, I believe God then places a sign out there that says, NO FISHING ALLOWED."

The solemn faces stared back at me, not quite daring to believe. There were never questions after a talk in Germany in 1947. People stood up in silence, in silence collected their wraps, in silence left the room.

And that's when I saw him, working his way forward against the others. One moment I saw the overcoat and the brown hat; the next, a blue uniform and a visored cap with its skull and crossbones. It came back with a rush: the huge room with its harsh overhead lights; the pathetic pile of dresses and shoes in the center of the floor; the shame of walking naked past this man. I could see my sister's frail form ahead of me, ribs sharp beneath the parchment skin. Betsie, how thin you were!

The man who was making his way forward had been a guard—one of the most cruel guards.

Now he was in front of me, hand thrust out: "A fine message, Fraulein! How good it is to know that, as you say, all our sins are at the bottom of the sea!"

And I, who had spoken so glibly of forgiveness, fumbled in my pocketbook rather than take that hand. He would not remember me, of course—how could he remember one prisoner among those thousands of women?

But I remembered him and the leather crop swinging from his belt. I was face-to-face with one of my captors and my blood seemed to freeze.

"You mentioned Ravensbruck in your talk," he was saying. "I was a guard there." No, he did not remember me.

"But since that time," he went on, "I have become a Christian. I know that God has forgiven me for the cruel things I did there, but I would like to hear it from your lips as well. Fraulein,"—again the hand came out—"will you forgive me?"

I stood there—I whose sins had again and again been forgiven—and could not forgive. Betsie had died in that place—could he erase her slow terrible death simply for the asking?

It could not have been many seconds that he stood there—hand held out—but to me it seemed like hours as I wrestled with the most difficult thing I had ever had to do.

For I had to do it—I knew that. The message that God forgives has a prior condition: that we forgive those who have injured us. "If you do not forgive men their trespasses," Jesus says, "neither will your Father in heaven forgive your trespasses."

I knew it not only as a commandment of God, but as a daily experience. Since the end of the war, I had a home in Holland for victims of Nazi brutality. Those who were able to forgive their former enemies were able also to return to the outside world and rebuild their lives, no matter what the physical scars. Those who nursed their bitterness remained invalids. It was as simple and as horrible as that.

And still I stood there with the coldness clutching my heart. But forgiveness is not an emotion—I knew that too. Forgiveness is an act of the will, and the will can function regardless of the temperature of the heart. "Jesus, help me!" I prayed silently. "I can lift my hand. I can do that much. You supply the feeling."

And so woodenly, mechanically, I thrust my hand into the one stretched out to me. And as I did, an incredible thing took place. The current started in my shoulder, raced down my arm, sprang into our joined hands. And then this healing warmth seemed to flood my whole being, bringing tears to my eyes.

"I forgive you, brother!" I cried. "With all my heart." For a long moment we grasped each other's hands, the former guard and the former prisoner. I had never known God's love so intensely as I did then. But even so, I realized it was not my love. I had tried, and did not have the power. It was the power of the Holy Spirit as recorded in Romans 5:5, ". . . because the love of God is shed abroad in our hearts by the Holy Ghost which is given unto us."[2]

Personalizing These Principles

1. Have I allowed bitterness to capture my soul because someone has treated me unjustly?

   God says, "Get rid of all bitterness, rage and anger, brawling and slander, along with every form of malice. Be kind and compassionate to one another, forgiving each other, just as in Christ God forgave you" (Eph. 4:31–32).

2. Have I allowed my bitterness toward others to become bitterness toward God?

   God says, "And we know that in all things God works for the good of those who love him, who have been called according to his purpose. . . . Who shall separate us from the love of Christ? Shall trouble or hardship or persecution or famine or nakedness or danger or sword? . . . No, in all these things we are more than conquerors through him who loved us" (Rom. 8:28, 35, 37).

3. Have I become vindictive toward those who have mistreated me, seeking to get even?

   God says, "Do not repay anyone evil for evil. . . . Do not take revenge, my friends, but leave room for God's wrath, for it is written: 'It is mine to avenge; I will repay,' says the Lord. . . . Do not be overcome by evil, but overcome evil with good" (Rom. 12:17, 19, 21).

Set a Goal

Now that you have read over the questions to help you personalize these principles we've learned from Joseph's life, take another step. Set a personal goal. For example, you may have allowed anger to turn into bitterness and it's withering your soul. It's affecting everything you do in a negative way. You can't even worship God with a free conscience. Set a goal to help you overcome this bitterness, which may involve asking forgiveness—in spite of what someone may have done to you that is wrong. Write out your particular goal:

_____

_____

_____

_____

Memorize the Following Scripture

Do not repay anyone evil for evil. Be careful to do what is right in the eyes of everybody. If it is possible, as far as it depends on you, live at peace with everyone. . . . Do not be overcome by evil, but overcome evil with good.

ROMANS 12:17–18, 21

Growing Together

The following questions are designed for small group discussion:

1. How have you kept normal anger from turning into bitterness?

2. How have you come to know God better in the midst of adversity? Could you share the process you went through emotionally and spiritually?

3. Could you share an experience where you've been able to "overcome evil with good"?

4. Perhaps you're struggling from what you consider unfair and unjust treatment. How can we help you through this painful process?

5. What personal prayer needs do you have?

Chapter 6

The Pain of Patience
Read Genesis 40:23–41:40

*O*ne of the difficult moments in life is to be patient when we want something to happen and we can't do anything about it—except wait! Unfortunately, life is filled with these "moments." It's a reality of life.

However, the pain that accompanies patience intensifies even more when we find ourselves in a position of being misunderstood and maligned—and we are unable to defend ourselves without creating more misunderstanding.

In the last chapter, I shared a personal experience that involved these very dynamics. Falsely accused, there was little I could do to clarify the situation. I simply had to wait and trust the Lord to vindicate my reputation. As you remember, He did! When one of these key men was sentenced to prison, the truth finally came out! But in the process, several years passed by—very painful years. I had only one choice—to wait and be patient. It was one of the greatest learning experiences of my life.

Two Long Years

One of the great virtues God was developing in Joseph's life was patience. You'll need to read the last verse in chapter 40 of

Genesis and the first verse in chapter 41 to experience the full impact of what must have happened in Joseph's heart and mind when he had to wait another two years to be vindicated. We read that "the chief cupbearer, however, did not remember Joseph; *he forgot him.*" And *"when two full years had passed,* Pharaoh had a dream" (40:23, 41:1).

A Ray of Hope

When Joseph interpreted the cupbearer's dream, reassuring him that he would be reinstated to his former position, he asked this high-ranking official to put in a good word for him to the king. This must have been Joseph's first ray of hope for release since his confinement to prison by Potiphar several years before. Joseph certainly saw this opportunity as an answer to his prayers. After all, he had not allowed bitterness to grip his soul, and he had fulfilled his duties faithfully without complaining.

Every day since his encounter with the cupbearer and the chief baker, he had waited for some word, for some indication that Pharaoh was concerned about him. After all, if the cupbearer had told the whole story, Pharaoh would have known that Joseph had interpreted his dream accurately. Surely Pharaoh would be interested in discovering more about Joseph's ability, since it was not something new for the king to consult magicians and wise men who could predict the future.

Hanging On by Faith

But no word came. Days turned into weeks and weeks into months and months into two full years! What hope he had must have faded. Remember that God had not revealed to Joseph what was going to happen. The fact that he had a supernatural gift to predict someone else's future did not mean that he had the same ability to predict his own. Joseph had to continue his prison experience by faith.

Fortunately, Joseph had hope beyond hope. That's what kept him from despair all during this terrible ordeal. His faith was in God, not in Potiphar, not in the cupbearer, not even in the king of Egypt. When men failed him, he knew God was still with him, even in prison. This is what enabled him to endure in the midst of deep sorrow and distress.

In this sense, Jacob could identify with Job. Job lost every-thing—including his children. Eventually his close friends turned against him and his wife told him to "curse God and die!" (Job 2:9). Job's response is classic. "'You are talking like a foolish woman,'" he replied. "'Shall we accept good from God, and not trouble?'" And then we read, "In all this, Job did not sin in what he said" (2:10).

Joseph, like Job, accepted what was happening to him even though he didn't understand it. He never gave up hope—although I am sure he spent many hours in deep sorrow and debilitating depression.

Nostalgic Memories

Joseph certainly wanted to be free from prison. But more than anything, he missed his family in Canaan. He made this clear to the cupbearer, at least by implication, when he said, "'I was forcibly carried off from the land of the Hebrews'" (40:15). In other words, he was saying, "I don't really belong here. I was brought here against my will. I want to go home."

Think for a moment about Joseph's family relationships. When he encountered the cupbearer and chief baker, it had been eleven long years since he had seen his father, the man to whom he had been so close. He was Jacob's favorite son. And Joseph's last visual memory of his dad was when Jacob had so naively sent him—clothed in his royal robe—to check on his brothers in Shechem.

Since Joseph was such a sensitive man, he had grieved deeply for his father who was told that he had been devoured by a wild animal. Think how often he must have wanted to send a message to his father that he was still alive. Better yet, how wonderful it would be to make a sudden appearance and surprise Jacob—that is, if he were still alive. Joseph longed to go home.

Some Personal Reflections

Homesickness is real no matter what our age. I remember when I was a young boy I had my first experience being away from my family for two whole weeks. I was visiting one of my favorite uncles. One evening at the end of the first week, I was attending a special prayer service. While the people were singing and praying, the most awful feeling came over me. I began to weep, first softly and then uncontrollably. No matter what I did to try to stop, I couldn't. For at least an hour, I really didn't understand what was happening, and neither did the other folks in the room. I think some of them thought I was under conviction of sin! In retrospect, I now know I was homesick. I missed my family so desperately I thought I was going to die. And remember, it was only two weeks—not eleven years!

I also remember the long summers I spent a thousand miles away from my wife and children when I was doing graduate work at New York University. Though I was very busy with my studies, I dreaded weekends. There I was in the middle of New York City, strolling across Washington Square Park or meandering through Greenwich Village. People were everywhere, but I felt like the loneliest man in the world. I missed my family terribly—even though I could write and receive letters. I could also use the telephone, and I could fellowship with other Christians. Even so, I was incredibly lonely.

Think for a moment how Joseph must have felt. He was completely shut away from his family for years. He had no opportunity to communicate. Humanly speaking, there was no way out of this desperate plight.

Pharaoh's Two Dreams

Dreams played a very important part in Joseph's life. Many years before, it was his own dreams that made his brothers terribly jealous and angry. It was those dreams that caused them to sell him as a slave to the Midianite merchants (37:19–20). And now, years later, it was his God-given ability to interpret dreams that would secure his release from prison and bring a promotion that would affect not only his destiny, but the destiny of the Egyptians, the destiny of his own family, and the destiny of Israel as a nation (41:1–8).

"Two full years" after the cupbearer had been reinstated—probably again on Pharaoh's birthday—the king had a dream. He saw seven well-fed cows grazing in the Nile River. Then he saw seven undernourished cows come up out of the Nile. They immediately devoured the seven well-fed cows (41:1–4).

Chances are, Pharaoh wasn't too puzzled about this first dream. However, he had a second dream. This time seven healthy heads of grain were devoured by seven "thin and scorched" heads of grain (41:5–7). When Pharaoh awakened after this second dream, he was deeply "troubled."

Pharaoh immediately saw the similarities and contrasts in the two dreams. In both dreams there was a "set of sevens" followed by a second "set of sevens." The first set of sevens involved *prosperity* and the second set of sevens involved a *lack of prosperity*—an obvious contrast. But similarly, the second set of sevens in both dreams that lacked prosperity devoured the first "set of sevens" that were prosperous.

If Pharaoh had reflected carefully—which he must have done—he would have also noticed that the first dream involved a *pastoral setting* and the second an *agricultural setting*—which involved both a similarity and a contrast. One dream involved the *flocks of Egypt* and the second the *crops of Egypt*. Together, these two aspects of the economy represented the lifeblood of Egypt.

| PHARAOH'S TWO DREAMS ||
Similarities	Contrasts
Two Sets of Seven	Prosperity—Lack of Prosperity
Second Set of Seven Triumphed	Pastoral Setting— Agricultural Setting
Flock—Crops	

No wonder Pharaoh was troubled! Like the cupbearer's and chief baker's dreams, the king realized his experience was more than bizarre, subconscious thinking. Consequently, "he sent for all the magicians and wise men of Egypt." He explained his dreams, but "no one could interpret them" (41:8). These men must have tried desperately to discover a satisfactory meaning in order to please the king, but Pharaoh knew that they did not have the answers to his questions.

A Jolted Memory

This process must have taken weeks. Day after day the magicians and wise men of Egypt came and went, leaving the king more troubled and frustrated each time. But watching all of this was the cupbearer, who, at some point in time remembered his own experience with Joseph. Or perhaps he gained enough courage to talk about what he had forced himself to forget. Whatever his thoughts, he came to Pharaoh and said, "'Today I am reminded of my shortcomings'" (41:9). It appears he actually felt guilty for not remembering Joseph's request two years before.

The cupbearer recounted the time he spent in prison as a result of Pharaoh's anger. He also told the king about this "young Hebrew" who was there. He probably had even forgotten Joseph's name, but he remembered he had been a servant of Potiphar. "'We told him our dreams,'" the cupbearer continued, "'and he interpreted them for us, giving each man the interpretation of his dream'" (41:12).

What must have impressed Pharaoh most was the fact that "things turned out exactly" as Joseph had stated they would (41:13). He immediately "sent for Joseph" (41:14), who was released from the dungeon and given opportunity to shave and change his clothes. He then appeared before Pharaoh.

Joseph's Great Opportunity!

Pharaoh related to Joseph that he had no one who could interpret his dreams. "'But,'" he said, "'I have heard it said of

you that when you hear a dream you can interpret it'"
(41:15).

Joseph's response indicates the man of God he truly was.
How easy it would have been to try to impress Pharaoh with
his own abilities. After all, this was his big opportunity! He
was standing before the king of Egypt! If he could prove himself to Pharaoh, he might be released from prison.

But Joseph took absolutely no credit for what had happened
two years before. "'I cannot do it,' Joseph replied to Pharaoh,
'but *God will give Pharaoh the answer* he desires'" (41:16).

We can now see even more clearly why both Potiphar and
the prison warden were so impressed with Joseph's abilities.
All along they had seen a direct correlation between the God
he worshiped and the success he enjoyed. Joseph had openly
honored the Lord for his achievements and successes. He took
no credit for himself.

Pharaoh was impressed more than ever. He trusted Joseph
and related his two dreams (41:17–24). And just as he had
done two years before, Joseph gave an instant interpretation.
There were no incantations, no religious exercises, no pagan
practices—as the magicians would have done. He simply and
succinctly told Pharaoh the meaning of both dreams.

"'The dreams of Pharaoh are one and the same,'" Joseph
reported. Furthermore, "'God has revealed to Pharaoh what he
is about to do'" (41:25).

Joseph then went on to interpret the dreams. The first sets
of seven referred to "seven years of *great abundance*" and the
second sets of seven referred to "seven years of *famine.*" And to
make sure Pharaoh really understood the seriousness of the
prediction, Joseph told him that "the reason the dream was
given . . . in two forms" was so that Pharaoh would know that
what was definitely going to happen had been "firmly decided
by God" and that it would happen "soon" (41:32).

Pharaoh's mind and heart had been prepared for Joseph's
interpretation. He had already concluded that his two dreams
were in reality only one (41:15). This is no doubt why he told
Joseph he had only one dream (41:15). Perhaps he had drawn

JOSEPH'S INTERPRETATION	
Two Dreams: "One and the Same"	
First "Sets of Seven" (Prosperity)	First Seven Years (Abundance)
Second "Sets of Seven" (Lack of Prosperity)	Second Seven Years (Famine)
"Firmly Decided by God" "God Will Do It Soon"	

this conclusion from his own reflections, or his wise men may have pointed out the obvious similarities. But now all the pieces fell into place in his mind.

Remember, too, that Pharaoh would have done a very careful background check on Joseph before he even brought him into his court. He certainly knew about his faithful service, both in Potiphar's house as well as in prison. He knew about his successes—and probably had heard directly from Potiphar what happened in his own household. Frankly, I believe Potiphar may have related the *true* story to the king—that Joseph was really an innocent man.

Pharaoh, then, was aware that he was not dealing with just an ordinary young man. All of Joseph's faithful efforts, his positive attitudes, and his unwavering trust in God over the last thirteen years were now paying significant dividends.

Joseph's Brave Proposal

Joseph was wise enough to also see unfolding before him a plan that God had designed all along (41:33–36). He knew that Pharaoh was listening intently and was open to suggestions. Consequently, he made a very wise—and brave—proposal: "'And now let Pharaoh look for a discerning and wise man and put him in charge of the land of Egypt'" (41:33).

Was Joseph thinking of himself when he made this proposal? Did he know in his heart that he would be the man who should be put "in charge of the land of Egypt"? Had God revealed to him that this is one of the major reasons he was sold into Egypt?

The text in Scripture doesn't spell out the answers to these questions at this point in time. However, we do know that after God used Joseph to not only save Egypt from disaster but to save his own family from starvation, Joseph *did* understand God's plan clearly (50:15–21). My personal opinion, however, is that God made this point rather clear to Joseph while he was in the process of interpreting Pharaoh's dreams. I believe that he suddenly saw that he was the man that God was preparing to navigate the Egyptian government through the coming economic storm.

But I also believe something else happened to Joseph. How could he help but remember his own dreams as a seventeen-year-old—dreams that he so naively shared with his brothers and which created such terrible anger and jealousy. But Joseph is now older and wiser. Whatever he knew in his heart at that moment, he wasn't about to make the same mistake twice by blurting out that he was to be Pharaoh's savior! Though his suggestion was very direct, it was also very subtle and discreet. He knew it would be incredibly presumptuous to suggest, even by implication, that he—a prisoner in Pharaoh's dungeon—should be elevated to this kind of position in the Egyptian kingdom.

From Prison to Palace

Pharaoh responded positively to Joseph's plan (41:37–40). Not only was he impressed with the proposal, but he knew who the man should be. It was none other than Joseph. Turning to his officials, he asked, "'Can we find anyone like this man, one in whom is the spirit of God?'"—indicating that he understood clearly that Joseph's capabilities were supernatural (41:38). He also saw Joseph's capabilities against the backdrop of the efforts of all the other magicians and wise men of Egypt. Joseph stood head and shoulders above them all!

Think for a moment what God had designed. Had Joseph come before Pharaoh two years before, chances are it would have been only because of the king's curiosity. There would have been no personal need or sense of urgency in his own heart. He would not have called for all the wise men of Egypt. Consequently, there would have been no opportunity for Pharaoh to compare Joseph's success with their failure. This is why he said to Joseph, "'There is no one so discerning and wise as you'" (41:39).

The extent of Pharaoh's trust is clear. Joseph suddenly went from prison to palace—not only to live there, but to have authority over the whole kingdom of Egypt. Thus Pharaoh said, "'Only with respect to the throne will I be greater than you'" (41:40). What a remarkable, incredible, and ironic development!

Becoming God's Man Today

Principles to Live By

Principle 1. *Learning to wait patiently strengthens our confidence in God without reducing the self-confidence we need to function in life.*

Joseph did not lack self-confidence. If anything, at age seventeen, he probably had too much. Or perhaps more accurately, he had not balanced it properly with confidence in God. If he had, he would have been more cautious in how he shared his dreams with his family. However, through all of Joseph's difficulties there is no evidence that he ever lost his self-confidence. Conversely, he developed his God-confidence.

How clear this was when he emerged from prison to stand before Pharaoh. Had he lacked self-confidence on the one hand, or had he been overconfident on the other, he would have tried to impress Pharaoh with his own abilities. But Joseph's response was in essence, "I cannot do it, but God can." Joseph had believed it two years earlier when he first met the king's cupbearer and baker (40:8), but two years of waiting had only convinced Joseph even more.

Men and women of God who are forced to live in circumstances that are totally beyond their control emerge knowing more than ever before that, without God, they can do nothing. Their faith, though "refined by fire," comes forth like gold. It's "proved genuine" (1 Pet. 1:7). At the same time, their self-confidence develops but is focused in Jesus Christ. With Paul they can say, "I have been crucified with Christ and I no longer live, but Christ lives in me. The life I live in the body, I live by faith in the Son of God, who loved me and gave himself for me" (Gal. 2:20).

Principle 2. A period of waiting often allows time for us to develop true character and to reflect that character to others.

Again, how true this was in Joseph's life. Though he must have wavered often, he never turned away from God. He weathered every storm. Though tempted to be bitter, immoral, and proud, he never let down his guard. How else could these qualities have been developed and revealed?

And how true in a Christian's life! There are things we cannot learn apart from a period of waiting, and often that period must be in a context of adversity. I've seen this happen in the lives of many men I've had the privilege of discipling over the years. Some have faced incredible difficulties—some of which I'm not sure I could handle in my own life. And yet, in the midst of these adversities, they've only grown closer to God. Though they've sometimes wavered and regressed, I've seen them bounce back, more determined than ever to reflect God's character in their lives—to be more committed to "measure up to the stature of the fullness of Jesus Christ."

Take Jim for instance. He had a terribly dysfunctional family. He was abandoned by his parents and lived in an orphanage. He didn't even know when his birthday was until he was twelve years old—which means no one ever celebrated this special day in his life.

But Jim survived. He became a Christian in his twenties, and he became a very successful businessman. Unfortunately, he made some bad judgments that led him into a world of business that violated his values. Guilt-ridden, he resigned as CEO of a multi-million-dollar operation—and then faced a heartrending divorce.

Though Jim struggled, made more mistakes, and experienced almost unbearable loneliness, I saw him begin to grow spiritually. He refocused his life on Jesus Christ. Character weaknesses became strengths. His period of "wilderness wanderings" and having to wait for deliverance from some "prison-like" experiences developed spiritual qualities in his life he probably never would have realized otherwise. Jim, of course, is still in process—like all of us. But God is at work in his life, developing character.

Principle 3. A period of waiting often creates opportunities for advancement that may not happen otherwise.

God's timing was perfect in Joseph's life. And because it was, Joseph was not only released from prison but promoted by Pharaoh to the highest position in the kingdom.

This principle can be true in our own lives—if we are patient and wait for God's timing. Though our opportunities may be far more limited in scope than Joseph's, they will be there. Our temptation is to get in a hurry—especially if everything is not going our way. Perhaps God is saying, "Wait, and if you do, what I have for you will be far greater than anything you can create for yourself!"

This principle of waiting, of course, is not an excuse for inactivity, laziness, or indecisiveness. Joseph never rationalized his circumstances. In fact, his self-confidence and inner motivation were very obvious when he suggested to the king that he needed a wise man to oversee the Egyptian economy, knowing full well that the king would probably conclude that he, Joseph, was that man. But he took that step only when he knew in his heart that God's "red light" had turned "green."

Principle 4. A period of difficulty and pain helps us develop wisdom we otherwise might not have.

At the age of seventeen, Joseph was naive and tended to be prideful. Somehow he thought his brothers should have understood his dreams—that they would someday bow down to him. But thirteen years later, he was able to respond to Pharaoh with great wisdom and humility that was far beyond his years.

And so it is in our own Christian lives. If we can see adversity—even false accusations and false treatment—as an opportunity for growth, it can enable us to develop wisdom and judgment far beyond our own years!

Corrie Speaks Again

In her book *Tramp for the Lord,* Corrie ten Boom describes her feelings the day she was miraculously released from a Nazi concentration camp. In many respects, she and Joseph had a lot in common:

> When you are dying—when you stand at the gate of eternity—you see things from a different perspective than when you think you may live for a long time. I had been standing at that gate for many months, living in Barracks 28 in the shadow of the crematorium. Every time I saw the smoke pouring from the hideous smokestacks I knew it was the last remains of some poor woman who had been with me in Ravensbruck. Often I asked myself, "When will it be my time to be killed or die?"
>
> But I was not afraid. Following Betsie's death, God's Presence was even more real. Even though I was looking into the valley of the shadow of death, I was not afraid. It is here that Jesus comes the closest, taking our hand, and leading us through.
>
> One week before the order came to kill all the women of my age, I was free. I still do not understand all the details of my release from Ravensbruck. All I know is, it was a miracle of God.
>
> I stood in the prison yard—waiting the final order. Beyond the walls with their strands of barbed wire stood the silent trees

of the German forest, looking so much like the gray-green sets on the back of one of our theater stages in Holland.

Mimi, one of the fellow prisoners, came within whispering distance. "Tiny died this morning," she said without looking at me. "And Marie also."

Tiny! "Oh, Lord, thank You for letting me point her to Jesus who has now ushered her safely into Your Presence." And Marie. I knew her well. She lived in my barracks and had attended my Bible talks. Like Tiny, Marie had also accepted Jesus as her Lord. I looked back at the long rows of barracks. "Lord, if it was only for Tiny and Marie—that they might come to know You before they died—then it was all worthwhile."

A guard spoke harshly, telling Mimi to leave the yard. Then he said to me, "Face the gate. Do not turn around."

The gate swung open and I glimpsed the lake in front of the camp. I could smell freedom.

"Follow me," a young girl in an officer's uniform said to me. I walked slowly through the gate, never looking back. Behind me I heard the hinges squeak as the gate swung shut. I was free, and flooding through my mind were the words of Jesus to the church at Philadelphia: "Behold, I have set before thee an open door, and no man can shut it. . . ." (Revelation 3:8).[1]

Personalizing These Principles

Today, right now, you may be facing a difficult period in your own life—a period of anxious waiting. Ask yourself the following questions.

1. How can I use this experience to develop my confidence and faith in God? God says, "Consider it pure joy, my brothers, whenever you face trials of many kinds, because you know that the testing of your faith develops perseverance. Perseverance must finish its work so that you may be mature and complete, not lacking anything" (Jas. 1:2–4).

2. Is God using this experience to develop and reveal my character? God says, "Not only so, but we also rejoice in our sufferings, because we know that suffering produces perseverance; perseverance, character; and character, hope" (Rom. 5:3–4).

3. Is God using this experience to provide an opportunity to use me sometime in the future far more than He could at the present time? God says, "And we know that in all things God works for the good of those who love him, who have been called according to his purpose" (Rom. 8:28).

4. Is God using this experience to help me develop wisdom that will enable me to fill a role far beyond my own capabilities at the present time? God says, "If we are distressed, it is for your comfort and salvation; if we are comforted, it is for your comfort, which produces in you patient endurance of the same sufferings we suffer. And our hope for you is firm, because we know that just as you share in our sufferings, so also you share in our comfort" (2 Cor. 1:6–7).

Set a Goal

As you review these principles, focus on the one that is most relevant to your experiences at this moment in your life. For example, you may have difficulty finding positive meaning in your present experience. When you select a particular principle, translate it into a personal goal that you can begin to practice immediately:

_____

_____

_____

_____

_____

Memorize the Following Scripture

Praise be to the God and Father of our Lord Jesus Christ, the Father of compassion and the God of all comfort, who comforts us in all our troubles, so that we can comfort those in any trouble with the comfort we ourselves have received from God.
2 Corinthians 1:3–4

Growing Together

The following questions are designed for small group discussion:

1. How have you been able to use adverse circumstances and experiences to develop your own confidence and faith in God?

2. What character qualities has God developed in your own life through adversity and difficult situations?

3. Has God used a period of adversity to give you an opportunity to help someone else?

4. Why is it that so often it takes adverse circumstances to help us function in life with more wisdom?

5. What personal prayer requests would you like to share with the group?

Chapter 7

_____

A Divine Mosaic
Read Genesis 41:41–57

One of my most enjoyable experiences is to drive over a mountain pass that consists of dozens of switchbacks. A favorite of mine is Cook City Highway in Montana. When I lived for two years in Billings a number of years ago, I must have driven over this pass a dozen times.

As you ascend, you can periodically pull off the highway, stop, and look back. There, winding down the mountain and into the valley below, is a ribbon of road curving around a series of switchbacks. As you once again enter the main road and continue your climb, all you can see is the road a few hundred yards ahead and behind. But as you reach each "lookout," you can see the panorama and pattern below. Passing through the quaint mountain town of Big Timber, you finally reach an 11,000-foot summit.

You can see where you have come from and where you are going. You can see the big picture. It's an awesome experience.

Many of us have come to some point in our journey through life when we can look back and gradually, or perhaps somewhat suddenly, see a distinct pattern that we have not seen before.

The events in our lives—particularly the painful ones—make sense for the first time. As Christians, we see a divine mosaic. God has been at work in our lives, even when we didn't

_____

realize it. At that moment, we can even catch a glimpse into the future—what it may be in view of what has happened in the past.

Joseph reached this point in his life when Pharaoh promoted him to serve as prime minister of Egypt. Though he may have caught glimpses of some supernatural meaning in his difficult and painful thirteen-year experience, God's divine pattern for his life must have come into focus rather suddenly when he was promoted so quickly and so dramatically. Rarely does any person who is a foreigner released from prison—even when innocent—suddenly become a primary ruler of one of the most significant and affluent kingdoms in the world.

"I Hereby Put You in Charge"

Once Pharaoh witnessed Joseph's supernatural ability to interpret dreams and discovered the management skills he had demonstrated so faithfully both in Potiphar's house and in prison, he wasted no time in officially releasing him from prison and promoting him to a very lofty and responsible position in Egypt. "'I hereby put you *in charge* of the whole land of Egypt,'" he said to Joseph (41:41).

To be put "in charge" of something was not a new experience for Joseph. Potiphar had "put him *in charge* of his household" (39:4). The warden had "put Joseph *in charge* of all those held in the prison" (39:22). And now Pharaoh put him "*in charge* of the whole land of Egypt" (41:41).

Joseph's promotion is overwhelming and almost breathtaking. One day he was a Hebrew slave serving an open-ended prison sentence. The next day he was in Pharaoh's court, interpreting his dreams, giving him wisdom and advice. And before the day was out, Pharaoh assigned Joseph to the highest position in the Egyptian government—outside of being the king himself.

The privileges, power, and prestige that went with this promotion accentuate why this event is so dramatic and incredible, and indeed a miracle of God.

- **Geographical Control.** Joseph was responsible for "the *whole* land of Egypt"—a nation in ancient history comparable in influence and size only to the Babylonian Empire. Egypt's wealth was limitless.

- **Financial Authority.** "Pharaoh took his *signet* ring . . . and put it on Joseph's finger" (41:42). This gave Joseph an unlimited budget. With the king's ring, he could stamp any invoice, authorize any expenditure, and pay any amount to carry out the king's business.

- **Social Prestige.** Pharaoh dressed Joseph in royal garments. He provided him with a kingly wardrobe, and each garment was made of "fine linen"—the most exquisite fabric in all of Egypt. Furthermore, he "put a gold chain around his neck" (41:42). We can safely assume its size and value were commensurate with Joseph's new position.

- **Royal Privileges.** Pharaoh provided Joseph with his own private chariot—comparable to a presidential limousine in our culture today. Being second-in-command, he was assigned a group of men who rode ahead of him and cleared the way (41:43). Like any high government official, he had his own security force. In addition, these men made sure these people honored Joseph's presence, insisting that they "bow the knee" before him (KJV).

- **Political Power.** Joseph's greatest honor came when Pharaoh informed him that he as king would not even make a decision regarding Egyptian affairs without Joseph's advice and approval. "'I am Pharaoh,'" he said, "'but without your word no one will lift hand or foot in all Egypt'" (41:44). Joseph became one of the most esteemed, most respected, and most powerful men in the world of his day.

- **Religious Position.** There are two final things mentioned in the biblical text which relate to Joseph's religious status.

First, Pharaoh changed his name to Zaphenath—Paneah (41:45). Inherent in the term nath is the idea that "God speaks and lives." Though in the minds of Egyptian priests this referred to one of their gods, it was Pharaoh's attempt at indicating that he believed and wanted others to believe that Joseph was no ordinary man. In his own pagan way, he was trying to acknowledge Joseph's God who had helped him interpret his dreams. Remember that in the religious life in Egypt, there was always room for another god.

Second, Pharaoh provided Joseph with a wife. Note that her name was "Asenath daughter of Potiphera, priest of On" (41:45). This man's full identity and position in Egypt is unknown. However, he was certainly involved in the religious system, and his daughter's name included the same idea as Joseph's new name. Again, nath (in the name Asenath) means "God speaks and lives." Together this couple not only represented the king of Egypt but deity as well. Their names would constantly remind people of their religious position in the kingdom.

Painful but Powerful Lessons

When Pharaoh promoted Joseph, he was only "thirty years old" (41:46). Few men have been given this kind of power and authority at so young an age. When they are, it often leads to arrogance, irresponsible behavior, and a downfall. There are some exceptions of course—and Joseph was one of those exceptions.

But this leads us to some very important observations. The crazy-quilt pattern to this point in Joseph's life now began to take on meaning. Joseph's bizarre experiences suddenly turned into a beautiful tapestry in his heart and mind as memories—both pleasant and painful—flooded his soul. The last thirteen years of his life began to make sense; there was now rhyme and reason. What was often very painful during those years faded in his memory as he now understood God's purpose in allowing him to experience so much unjust treatment (41:51).

Let's look at how God prepared Joseph for his unique position in Egypt. What was God teaching him? Joseph learned some very painful lessons in at least three important areas: *pride, perseverance, and performance.*

Guarding against Pride

J. Oswald Sanders once wrote, "Not every man can carry a full cup. Sudden elevation frequently leads to pride and a fall. The most exacting test of all to survive is prosperity."

Since we know the overall story of Joseph's life, we also know he handled a "full cup" very well—in spite of his youthfulness. His "sudden elevation" to power did not lead to pride and a fall, but to even greater success and spirituality. He not only survived this test of prosperity but used it for the honor and glory of God.

This is a tribute to Joseph. But more so, his mature attitude points to what God had done in his life. The Lord had prepared Joseph well for this position. Thirteen years of very difficult experiences marked his life. He would not—and could not—forget the pit from which he came to Potiphar's house, or the prison that was his home for most of those years before he became the king's prime minister.

Joseph was a prime candidate for pride. He was a favorite son. He had a special place in his family from birth, even though he had ten brothers *older* than he. His father had given him a richly ornamented robe, signifying this special place. And at the tender age of seventeen, he had two dreams that verified his special place in the family and in God's divine plan (37:5–10).

Combined with all of these factors, Joseph was a very "well-built and handsome young man"—a factor alone that could lead the average man to be prideful. And certainly, his success also indicates his level of intelligence. Though he had at times supernatural mental powers, he certainly did not lack in I.Q.

Joseph was one of those men who had everything going for him, and it was all of these privileges and qualities that contributed to his success in Egypt. But first, he needed to be "refined by fire" and brought "forth as gold" (1 Pet. 1:7; Job 23:10). He needed this process to prepare him to handle the prestige and power that awaited him in Egypt.

God had great plans for Joseph, and He knew this young man would rise to the occasion only after being severely tested. Joseph passed each test satisfactorily all along the way. He did not become bitter. He had a forgiving spirit. He maintained a servant's heart. His self-confidence became properly balanced with God-confidence. And most of all, he never forgot the grace of God in sustaining him in his most trying years! God was weaving all of these factors into the fabric of his personality to help him guard against pride when suddenly elevated to his position in Egypt.

Learning to Persevere

There's a price tag on every high-level leadership position. Jealousy always rears its ugly head. At some point, most leaders encounter rumors, false accusations, misunderstandings, and breakdowns in communication.

Key leaders must also take responsibility for the mistakes of others. There will be sleepless nights and problems that can never be solved adequately. It's impossible to keep everyone happy. There will always be more to do than can be done. Unless prepared for these challenges, every man has difficulty persevering under this kind of pressure.

Joseph faced all of these problems. His responsibility was enormous. But perhaps his greatest stress came from the unconditional trust Pharaoh placed in him—and in his God! Joseph was under pressure to *not* fail his human master *or* his divine Master.

Fortunately, Joseph's preparation was also spiritual. With every difficulty, Joseph grew in his relationship with God. He learned to trust God. He saw God work on his behalf. Joseph knew the Lord would help him fulfill his task in Egypt—

enormous as it was. He had learned perseverance through thirteen years of very excruciating but highly profitable experience! Without it, he would not have been ready to handle the economic affairs of Egypt.

Facing a Demanding Task

The rest of chapter 41 spells out the seven years of plenty in Egypt and the beginning of the seven years of famine. Joseph's task called for superhuman wisdom and strength, especially for a young man in his thirties.

An Administrative Nightmare!

The "Seven Years of Plenty"

Throughout Egypt, Joseph supervised the gigantic storehouse operation (41:47–57). He "stored up huge quantities of grain, like the sand of the sea" in every city. In fact, the surplus became so great, Joseph "stopped keeping records." The biblical text states that the sheer quantity of grain "was beyond measure" (41:49). In addition to maintaining efficiency, think for a moment about the challenges Joseph faced just to guarantee honesty and integrity in this huge operation.

The "Seven Years of Famine"

When the predicted famine hit, Joseph faced the mammoth job of distribution. Maintaining equality would in itself be an administrative nightmare. If maintaining honesty and integrity were a problem the first seven years, think of what happened during the seven years of famine.

The full force of managing this operation lay squarely on Joseph's shoulders. When people began to come to Pharaoh for food, he "told all the Egyptians, 'Go to Joseph and do what he tells you'" (41:55).

This famine affected more than Egypt; it spread throughout the world. Joseph had to administer the distribution of food not only among the people of Egypt, but among those who came from other countries to buy food (41:56–57), including his own family in Canaan. What an enormous task!

Divine Preparation

At age thirty, Joseph could never have handled this world-class task without an intensive and experience-oriented course in management. It began in Potiphar's house, where he managed all of his affairs. It continued in prison where he was eventually responsible for all the prisoners. And thirteen years later, he was "put . . . in charge of the whole land of Egypt" (41:41).

God's plan for Joseph was on schedule. His preparation was tailor-made for the task God had for him. And because Joseph passed each test, learned from each experience, and learned to trust God more, he was ready when God opened the door of opportunity. He handled prestige and power without succumbing to pride. He persevered with patience and performed his duties faithfully and successfully. He was well prepared.

Becoming God's Man Today

Principles to Live By

What God taught Joseph, He wants to teach every one of us. True, few—if any of us—will ever be assigned a heavy task like Joseph. And fortunately, few of us will need the experiences Joseph needed to prepare us for our tasks! But we all need to learn the same things he did, no matter what our responsibilities and position in life.

Principle 1. God wants to teach us lessons that will help us avoid the pitfall of pride.

We all face this temptation. Joseph certainly did. And we all fail at times. But God cannot and will not use a Christian to the full who is prideful.

In the Book of Proverbs we read that "there are six things the LORD hates, seven that are detestable to him: haughty eyes, a lying tongue, hands that shed innocent blood, a heart that devises wicked schemes, feet that are quick to rush into evil, a false witness who pours out lies and a man who stirs up dissension among brothers" (Prov. 6:16–19).

At the top of this list is *pride*. This sin has destroyed the effectiveness of more Christians than any other and has kept many from rising to the level of responsibility God had in mind. But if we allow Him, He'll prepare us!

Pain Produces Humility

Samuel Rutherford once stated that we should "praise God for the hammer, the file, and the furnace." He went on to explain that the "hammer molds us, the file shapes us, and the fire tempers us." All three experiences are painful, but we can praise God for them because we know and love the God who wields them.

A. W. Tozer, commenting on Rutherford's statement, wrote, "The devil, things and people being what they are, it is necessary to use the hammer, the file and the furnace in the holy work of preparing the saint for the sainthood. It is doubtful whether God can bless a man greatly until he has hurt him deeply."[1]

Preparation Prevents Future Pain

In Joseph's life, all of the pain and humiliation that came his way would some day help him to face the temptation toward pride and be victorious! It would also help him avoid making prideful decisions that would bring even greater pain—namely, the pain that always accompanies failure.

Only a man prepared as Joseph was could have avoided falling prey to pride when suddenly given such an awesome position and power. God had Joseph's interests at heart, including all those who were impacted by his life.

Principle 2. *God wants to prepare us spiritually and emotionally to persevere as we face difficult responsibilities.*

I remember an experience in my own life that I *now* see as God's preparation. When I graduated from Moody Bible Institute, I was involved in a ministry which I considered a great privilege. But during this experience, I became very disappointed with several key Christian leaders. For several long months, I entered a very dark period in my life, primarily because of disillusionment. I took my eyes off the Lord and put them on men. I was so disillusioned I began to doubt my own salvation. I even wondered if there was a God. At times I was so miserable and disillusioned I was tempted to leave the ministry completely.

At the time all this was happening, I did not realize God allowed this experience to deal with some serious spiritual and emotional weaknesses in my own life. When I left that ministry and began graduate work at Wheaton College, I was suddenly given an opportunity to join the faculty at Moody Bible Institute. At the time, I was only twenty-three years old and was teaching some students that were older than I. It didn't take me long to see that my previous difficulties with pain had a purpose. In certain respects, it seems God put my learning experiences in "fast forward" in order to prepare me for this unique teaching opportunity. Without those dark days and learning to persevere through some very difficult circumstances, I would not have been able to endure and survive the tasks God opened for me.

In retrospect, I believe God gave me a choice during that difficult period. I could have left the ministry, as I was tempted to do. If I had, I might never have gone on to the next level of opportunity in God's service. It might have changed the whole direction of my life.

God gives all of us certain choices at various points along our journey in life. We can either persevere in the midst of difficulties and learn valuable lessons about ourselves and what it takes to persevere in even more demanding and stretching responsibilities, or we can choose to turn away and take what appears at the moment to be an easier way. In some instances, we may even turn aside from His perfect will.

As no other teacher, God knows exactly what curriculum we *each* need to both prepare us in specific areas of our personality and to also prepare us for specific tasks. We all need "the hammer, the file, and the furnace"! And if we pass each test along the way, God will advance us to another level in His great work on earth. On the other hand, if we want to settle for less, He'll honor our choice.

Principle 3. God wants to design a curriculum for each of us in order to prepare us to perform well *when given greater and greater responsibility.*

Greater pressure and the need for greater skills always accompany advancement. But with greater pressure also comes personal growth and more meaningful and lasting fruit in the kingdom of God—now and eternally. There is nothing more important in life than to do the will of God and to advance His work. Our personal comfort should always be a secondary consideration. After all, the Lord never promised us a rose garden on this earth. In fact, Jesus said, "'If anyone would come after me, he must deny himself and take up his cross and follow me'" (Matt. 16:24).

When we follow God fully, there are always marvelous rewards. But there are times we must pass through a valley to reach the next mountaintop in God's plan for our lives.

Personalizing These Principles

Think for a moment about the mosaic in your own life. As you reflect, can you see meaning in your past and present experiences? What is God doing to prepare you, to equip you, to conform you into His image?

Fortunately, we have Joseph's experience to guide us, and encourage us—plus the whole of Scripture. Even in the midst of darkness, we can see light because we know God loves us, that He will never forsake us and that, if we trust Him, we will "come forth as gold." Will you let Him guide and control your life?

When Joseph was promoted to prime minister in Egypt, he, in a sense, had reached the summit in God's plan for his life. Now both the past and the future made sense. Though many details in his future were still invisible and uncertain, God's overall mosaic was clear.

Can you believe that God will some day do the same for you? He will—if you let Him!

Steps to Success

1. You must acknowledge the sin that separates you and all of us from God. God says, "For all have sinned and fall short of the glory of God (Rom. 3:23). "For the wages of sin is death" (Rom. 6:23).

2. You must realize and understand that Jesus Christ paid the penalty for your sins and the sins of the whole world when He died on the cross. God says, "But God demonstrates his own love for us in this: While we were still sinners, Christ died for us" (Rom. 5:8). "'For God so loved the world that he gave his one and only Son, that whoever believes in him shall not perish but have eternal life'" (John 3:16).

3. You must receive Jesus Christ as your own personal Savior from sin. God says, "Yet to all who received him, to those who believed in his name, he gave the right to become children of God" (John 1:12). "For it is by grace you have been saved, through faith—and this not from yourselves, it is the gift of God—not by works, so that no one can boast" (Eph. 2:8–9).

4. You must make Jesus Christ Lord of your life. This means obeying His Word and trusting Him day by day in all circumstances. God says, "Trust in the LORD with all your heart and lean not on your own understanding; in all your ways acknowledge him, and he will make your paths straight" (Prov. 3:5–6).

Set a Goal

As you reflect back on the principles in this chapter, which one do you need to focus on?

> Do you allow pride to sidetrack you from doing God's will?

> Do you have difficulty persevering? Are you constantly tempted to bail out?

> Do you see God at work in your life preparing you for an even greater task?

Select the area most appropriate to your needs and write out a personal goal:

_____

_____

_____

_____

Memorize the Following Scripture

And we know that in all things God works for the good of those who love him, who have been called according to his purpose. For those God foreknew he also predestined to be conformed to the likeness of his Son, that he might be the firstborn among many brothers.

ROMANS 8:28–29

Growing Together

The following questions are designed for small group discussion:

1. Would you share how God prepared you for a special task?

2. More specifically, how has God dealt with your temptation to be prideful?

3. How has God helped you develop perseverance in carrying out your Christian responsibilities—in your family, in your church, and in your vocation?

4. Have you reached a "summit" in your life where you can now more clearly see God's divine mosaic? Would you feel free to share with us where you are in this unique process?

5. What can we pray for you specifically?

Chapter 8

Healing for Emotional Hurts
Read Genesis 41:50–52

*H*ave you ever been rejected by those you love—particularly those in your own family? I posed this question in my church one Sunday morning—only more specifically. I asked how many had actually been disowned by their families when they became Christians. Several hands went up. This must have been a painful experience.

What about false accusations from those you've always trusted? That can be even more painful. But most painful of all, have you ever been punished for something you didn't do? If you stop and reflect—and introspect—you may still feel some hurt, even though you've put those painful events behind you.

One of the most hurtful experiences for me as a pastor is when I've loved and served someone faithfully and unconditionally and they simply turn and walk away, never looking back. No matter how much I tell myself that this goes with the territory—and even though I remind myself that Jesus said it would happen—it still hurts!

Joseph's Emotional Pain

Joseph understood rejection from those he loved and served. However, his experiences were far more intense than anything most of us will ever have to endure. Think of the times he must have painfully reflected on that horrible day when his brothers stripped him of his ornamented robe and threatened to kill him. He also understood false accusations and being punished and put in shackles for something he didn't do. And to top it off, he was forgotten by a man he helped—the cupbearer to the king of Egypt. But in all of this, God did not forget Joseph, and Joseph did not allow bitterness to wrap its tentacles around his troubled soul. Nevertheless, he was just as human as anyone of us—and the emotional pain must have been almost more than he could bear.

How did God bring about mental and emotional healing in Joseph's heart and mind? To answer this question, let's reflect on his incredible promotion from prison to palace. God orchestrated several important factors that brought beautiful and harmonious music into his heart—a heart that had been filled with a cacophony of sounds and dissonance.

Free at Last!

The first step in Joseph's emotional healing is certainly related to his release from prison. For the first time in thirteen years, what had happened in his life began to make sense. He saw purpose in his suffering. Think how he must have felt when he was exonerated from a crime he didn't commit.

I believe that the truth came out regarding the false accusations against Joseph by Potiphar's wife. Remember that her servants were certainly privy to her scheme. They knew all about her deceitful and lustful heart—and when it comes to loyalty, "servants" stroke the hand that feeds them. People talk—and when the word was out that Joseph was put in charge of all Egypt, it wouldn't take long for these servants to transmit Joseph's innocence along the political grapevine.

While doing a search of Joseph's background—which Pharaoh certainly must have done—Pharaoh may have even discovered the truth before he made his decision to promote

Joseph to this prestigious position. Needless to say, all of this contributed significantly to Joseph's emotional healing. Not only was he free from prison, he was also free in his spirit. He needn't be concerned any longer about the false accusations against him.

Respect and Honor

Another factor in Joseph's healing involved his position—the way he was respected and honored. He went from being a prisoner that everyone looked down on to being a man everyone looked up to! Pharaoh trusted him totally—giving him absolute authority. "'Without your word,'" Pharaoh stated for all to hear, "'no one will lift hand or foot in all Egypt'" (41:44). As Joseph traveled throughout the land, everyone paid their respects. Those who went before him, actually shouted, "Make way!" More literally, people were told to "bow down" before Joseph. He received the same respect and honor as Pharaoh himself.

For a man who had been sold as a slave and then incarcerated in chains and shackles, this experience must have overwhelmed Joseph. It certainly contributed to his emotional healing. This kind of position and prestige would help any man forget the humiliating pain from the past.

But, in all of this, God had also prepared Joseph to cope with the temptation to be prideful. Nothing serves to remind us of the fallacy of becoming arrogant like a series of painful and humiliating events that cause memories and impressions we'll never forget. Often God prepares His servants for significant success by allowing periods of intense persecution and false accusations—or even failure because of our own mistakes. At this moment in Joseph's life, God restored his wounded spirit by giving him success beyond measure. And from this point forward, it appears that Joseph never succumbed to prideful behavior. Was he tempted? I'm sure he was—but he never forgot the "pit from which he was dug." This reflects true emotional and spiritual healing!

"Seven Years of Abundance!"

God granted Joseph instant success in his new role. His position in Egypt was reinforced by seven years of unusual abundance (41:47–49). The land produced "huge quantities of grain"—more so than ever before. His prophetic interpretation of Pharaoh's dream became a reality and everyone would have associated these bumper crops with Joseph himself.

The "success factor" was not a new experience for Joseph. In fact, "the LORD gave him *success* in everything he did" when he first served in Potiphar's house as a servant (39:3). And when he was sentenced to prison, the Lord also "gave him *success* in whatever he did" (39:23).

This was important in Joseph's ability to cope with the rejection he felt from his brothers and the pain he experienced from the false accusations against him by Potiphar's wife. No human being can survive this kind of deep emotional hurt without an element of success—especially when we're bombarded with painful experiences. But any success he experienced during the first thirteen years paled compared to the success he experienced as prime minister of Egypt. Needless to say, this helped Joseph "forget" the painful emotions associated with the past.

Marital Companionship

Another factor in Joseph's healing related to his marriage (41:45). Pharaoh provided him with a wife—no doubt a very special lady. Though Asenath was the daughter of a pagan priest, she certainly came to understand rather quickly that Joseph's God was the one true God. In fact, Pharaoh made it easy for people to believe in Joseph's God when he posed that penetrating question to his top advisors—"'Can we find anyone like this man, one in whom is the *spirit of God?*'" (41:37).

Reciprocal Love

Being the daughter of a priest, Asenath would probably find it easy to be married to a man who had a deep spiritual dimension—especially when she had the approval of Pharaoh himself. But more importantly for Joseph, this was the first time he had this kind of close companionship since he was so heartlessly separated from his father. Marriage provided him with an intimate experience that God designed to be unequaled in human relationships. He had someone to love and someone who would return his love. He had someone who would listen—someone who would understand his painful journey. Think of the hours Asenath must have spent listening to Joseph reflect on his past life.

A Supportive Wife

It's difficult to imagine that after so many difficulties and heartaches that God would allow Joseph to marry a woman who would make his life even more miserable. If that had happened, he would never have experienced emotional healing. And if he had not experienced emotional healing, he never would have been able to handle the superhuman task of directing the economic affairs of Egypt. All of his energy would have been diverted to trying to resolve his domestic problems.

It's sad when this happens in a marriage. Listen to the following proverbs: "Better to live in a desert than with a quarrelsome and ill-tempered wife" (Prov. 21:19). "A quarrelsome wife is like a constant dripping on a rainy day; restraining her is like restraining the wind or grasping oil with the hand" (27:15–16).

From the overall story of Joseph's life, I'm confident that these verses *do not* describe Asenath. She evidently was a very supportive wife. Her friendship and love helped bring healing to Joseph's soul.

A Moral Example

Though Asenath helped restore Joseph's emotional equilibrium, he was clearly her spiritual leader. He did not allow himself to be influenced by her pagan background. For one thing, she was the only woman in his life. In a pagan society and government where men in high government positions often demonstrated their power and prestige by the number of women in their harem, this is indeed significant. Joseph didn't even follow in the footsteps of his father, Jacob. He maintained a monogamous relationship all his life—knowing this was God's ideal plan for marriage. What an example this must have been in this pagan culture!

"A Heritage from the LORD"

After Joseph's promotion and "before the years of famine came," Asenath gave birth to two sons (Gen. 41:50). Note the names Joseph gave these two boys, and what these names meant (vv. 51–52). This is a significant clue for understanding more fully how God brought healing to Joseph's inner being. This experience also illustrates what Solomon wrote centuries later— "Sons are a heritage from the LORD, children a reward from him" (Ps. 127:3).

Manasseh—"God Has Made Me Forget"

Joseph named his first son *Manasseh,* literally meaning "one who causes to forget." He then explained why he chose this name—"'It is because God has made me *forget* all my trouble and all my father's household'" (Gen. 41:51). The connection is clear! There is a very definite cause-effect relationship between Manasseh's birth and Joseph's ability to *forget* his painful past.

What did Joseph mean? What did he forget?

➤ Did he forget the traumatic experience when he was rejected by his brothers?

➤ Did he forget that day when they stripped him of his richly ornamented robe and threw him into a pit?

➤ Did he forget the argument his brothers had regarding whether or not to take his life?

➤ Did he forget that horrible moment when they bartered with the Midianite merchants and finally settled on his price as a slave—twenty shekels of silver?

➤ Did he forget those days as he trudged wearily over the desert roads bound for a strange land, leaving his family far behind?

➤ Did he forget the slave block in Egypt where he was auctioned off to the highest bidder?

➤ Did he forget the daily experience of being exposed to sexual temptations by a seductive and sensuous woman?

➤ Did he forget this woman's cries of "rape, rape" when he ran away, refusing to violate his moral principles and his master's trust?

➤ Did he forget those long years in prison as an innocent man?

➤ Did he forget the cupbearer's failure to remember him when he was restored to Pharaoh's right hand?

➤ Did he forget those lonely hours thinking about his father and his deceased mother?

➤ Did he forget his little brother, Benjamin, who was only a young lad when Joseph was taken into captivity?

Joseph *never* forgot any of these events! How could he? The details were indelibly etched in his mind. If the events had been expunged from his memory, the overall experience would have been of little value. Furthermore, he wouldn't have mentioned his "trouble" and his "father's household" when Manasseh was born. In fact, he would have chosen a different name for his firstborn if he had forgotten altogether.

What, then, did God enable Joseph to forget through the birth of this little boy? It was the *pain* associated with those events. The emotional sting was gone. He was not in bondage to past experiences. There was no lingering bitterness, no inhibiting fear, no debilitating emotional sensitivity, and no obsessive thoughts, or compulsive behavior. Joseph had no regrets. God had healed his emotional memories.

Joseph now had two important people in his life—his wife, Asenath, and his firstborn, Manasseh. What a joyous day that must have been for Joseph! Just holding that little boy in his arms must have brought incredible emotional healing.

Ephraim—"God Has Made Me Fruitful"

Asenath bore Joseph a second son. Again, Joseph chose a name that focused on what God was doing in his life (41:52). *Ephraim* comes from a root word meaning "to be fruitful."

There are two possible interpretations regarding why Joseph named his second son Ephraim. By "fruitful," did he mean that God had given him a wife and two sons? Or was he referring to his position and accomplishments in Egypt? First and foremost, he was probably referring to his family. God had made him fruitful in giving him two sons. But God had also made him fruitful in giving him position, wealth, and success in Egypt. Joseph was in the midst of the "seven years of abundance" when his sons were born. The land "produced plentifully." Joseph had already "stored up huge quantities of grain, like the sand of the sea." There was "so much that he stopped keeping records because it was beyond measure" (41:47, 49). There's only one way to describe what was happening to Joseph both in his family life and in his political life. God had made him fruitful in the land of his "suffering."

With this statement, Joseph also let us know he had not forgotten what he suffered in Egypt. But he also let us know he was now rejoicing in what God had both allowed and done in his life. He understood both the trial and now his triumph. And his trial only served to make him stronger and more appreciative of God's present blessings and emotional healing in his life.

A Tribute

When I first studied the way in which God used Asenath and Joseph's two sons to bring emotional healing into his life, I determined I would not pass up this opportunity to pay tribute to my wife, Elaine—the mother of our three children. I wrote her a letter and surprised her by sharing it publicly with my "larger family"—the church where I serve as pastor. I want to share it with you—again to pay tribute to her—and if you're married, to also encourage you not to forget to honor the woman God gave you. Most of us would not be the men we are if it were not for our wives.

My dear Elaine,

It's very appropriate that I share this letter with you this morning—and publicly. So many times as a pastor's wife, you function behind the scenes and few people really know how faithful you are to me, and always have been. And I want everyone to know that without you—your *constant* support, your *encouragement,* your *devotedness* to me and to our children and to our grandchildren—I could not pastor and lead this church.

In fact, it's been that way for nearly forty years. I'm thankful particularly for those tough nine years when I was grinding out my doctorate at New York University—being away from you and the children during the summer months. I didn't realize until it was all over how difficult those years were for you. But you hung in there—uncomplaining. Thank you!

I think of our children. They're not perfect but I'm proud of them. And you are the reason. Without your commitment to them all these years, particularly picking up the slack when I've been overwhelmed with other people's problems, and often out of town or working late in the office, they would surely have become disillusioned with me—and Christianity. You've always defended me to them, interpreted my schedule, and reassured them of my love when I was absent or emotionally unable to be everything I wanted to be.

And thanks too for lovingly and boldly confronting me when I've failed to do the things I should have done. But thanks for always doing it face to face, never behind my back and never in front of the children.

I can identify with Joseph. You've often helped me *forget* my problems and you've been the primary secret to any *fruitfulness* in my life. I owe a great debt to you. Thank you!

With love and appreciation,
Gene

Becoming God's Man Today

Principles to Live By

Principle 1. All of us need a sense of "freedom," but the most important freedom God has provided is the freedom we can experience in Christ—no matter what our circumstances.

As Christians, we can experience a new sense of freedom at two levels. First, our personal salvation experience with Jesus Christ sets us free from the penalty and power of sin. Listen to these reassuring words from the apostle Paul: "Therefore, there is now no condemnation to those who are in Christ Jesus, because through Christ Jesus the law of the Spirit of life *set me free* from the law of sin and death" (Rom. 8:1–2).

Freedom from Sin's Power

As men who know Jesus Christ personally, we need not offer the parts of our bodies "in slavery to impurity and to ever-increasing wickedness" (6:19). Rather, since we are new creations in Christ Jesus (2 Cor. 5:17), we are *free* to offer our "bodies as living sacrifices, holy and pleasing to God" (Rom. 12:1). We have been "set free from sin and have become slaves to righteousness" (6:18).

Freedom to Love And Serve

As Christians, we also have a new sense of freedom in our relationships with other believers. Again, listen to the words of the apostle Paul: "You, my brothers, were *called to be free*. But do not use *your freedom* to indulge the sinful nature; rather, *serve one another in love* (Gal. 5:13).

People who are in bondage to sin are also in bondage to other human beings who "gratify the desires of the sinful nature" (5:16)—which involves "sexual immorality, impurity and debauchery; idolatry and witchcraft; hatred, discord, jealousy, fits of rage, selfish ambition, dissentions, factions and envy; drunkenness, orgies, and the like" (5:19–21).

This kind of lifestyle is not true freedom. People use and abuse one another. Relationships quickly become self-centered and vain. You can easily verify this by watching a few television talk shows. However, don't make it a habit or you'll find yourself indulging your own fleshly desires just listening and watching what the world even calls "trash T.V." There is no true freedom in the relationships talk show hosts exploit in order to gain an audience!

On the other hand, Christians who "live by the Spirit" and who "keep in step with the Spirit" (5:25) are free to "serve one another in love" (5:13), reflecting the "fruit of the Spirit"— which is, "love, joy, peace, patience, kindness, goodness, faithfulness, gentleness and self-control" (5:22–23). Rather than using our bondage to the flesh to manipulate others for our own ends, we can use our freedom in Christ to build others up. When we do, we'll be built up ourselves.[1] Unfortunately, these relationships never make the talk show agendas.

This kind of freedom within the body of Jesus Christ brings emotional healing. People who come from dysfunctional families can be "re-parented" by receiving unconditional love. They can learn the true meaning of love and in turn will be able to share that love with others. This is *true* freedom in Christ—no matter what our circumstances.

Principle 2. All of us need respect from others, but the most important factor is to be able to "respect ourselves" because we're living in the will of God.

Nothing brings more emotional healing in our lives than when we respect ourselves. And nothing brings more "self-respect" than when we "keep in step with the Spirit" (Gal. 5:25). Conversely, nothing is more self-destructive than to live under a cloud of guilt and self-condemnation that accompanies a sinful lifestyle.

I can identify with this principle—can't you? When I deliberately walk out of God's will, I lose self-respect. My emotional energy is devoted to fighting feelings of guilt and rationalizing my sinful behavior. My fellowship with God is broken and my relationships with other Christians are strained. This kind of "spiritual sickness" promotes "emotional sickness." The two cannot be separated. But, conversely, when I'm following God and walking in His will, I feel good about myself. My emotional energy is focused on pleasing God. What better place to be than in the "good, pleasing and perfect will of God" (Rom. 12:2).

Principle 3. All of us need to experience success, but the most important success we can experience is to have God's approval.

I know Christian men who have violated biblical values in order to be accepted by others—a boss, a friend, a marital partner. Though they may be successful by the world's standards, they're miserable people. Acceptance by others means virtually nothing when our behavior is not acceptable to God.

On the other hand, when we can lie down to sleep at night with a clear conscience knowing that God has been pleased with our attitudes and actions, what a blessed and rewarding experience! Nothing gives us more inner strength to face the challenges in life than a "pure heart and a good conscience and a sincere faith" (1 Tim. 1:5). Paul's later exhortation to Timothy applies to us all: "Do your best to present yourself to God *as one approved,* a workman who does not need to be ashamed and who correctly handles the word of truth" (2 Tim. 2:15).

Principle 4. All of us need companionship to overcome emotional hurts, but our most important companion is Jesus Christ.

Just before Jesus Christ returned to His Father, He gave His disciples a wonderful promise—"'And surely I am with you always, to the very end of the age'" (Matt. 28:20). This principle certainly applies to all of us. God in Jesus Christ and through the presence of the Holy Spirit has said, "'Never will I leave you; never will I forsake you'" (Heb. 13:5).

Joseph experienced God's abiding presence—even in an Old Testament setting. Though Jesus Christ had not come to earth yet, Joseph's heavenly Father—and ours—never forsook him. When his brothers sold him into Egypt, "the LORD was with him" (Gen. 39:3). When Pharaoh's wife falsely accused him and when Potiphar sentenced him to prison, "the LORD was with him" (39:21).

If this was true in Joseph's life, how much more so in the lives of those of us who have been redeemed by the blood of Christ and "marked in him with a seal, the promised Holy Spirit" (Eph. 1:13).

J. Wilbur Chapman captured the essence of this biblical principle when he wrote the lyrics to the wonderful hymn entitled "Our Great Savior"—

> Jesus! What a friend for sinners!
> Jesus! Lover of my soul;
> Friends may fail me, foes assail me,
> He, my Savior, makes me whole.
> Jesus! What a strength in weakness!
> Let me hide myself in Him;
> Tempted, tried, and sometimes failing,
> He, my strength, my vic-t'ry wins.
> Jesus! What a help in sorrow!
> While the billows o'er me roll,
> Even when my heart is breaking,
> He, my comfort, helps my soul.
> Jesus! What a guide and keeper!
> While the tempest still is high,
> Storms about me, night o'er takes me,
> He, my pilot, hears my cry.

Hallelujah! What a Savior!
Hallelujah! What a friend!
Saving, helping, keeping, loving,
He is with me to the end.

Principle 5. All of us need to experience the joy of having children in our lives, but we must remember that one of our greatest joys can come from having spiritual children.

As far as we know, the apostle Paul never had children of his own. However, he had many "spiritual children"—people he had led to Christ. But no one brought joy and healing to Paul's heart like Timothy. This great apostle "adopted" this young man as his missionary companion and identified him as his "true son in the faith" (1 Tim. 1:2).

When Paul wrote to the Philippians, he allowed all of us to peer into his soul and to catch a glimpse of how much Timothy's friendship and loyalty meant to him. Listen carefully to Paul's heartbeat: "I have no one else like him, who takes a genuine interest in your welfare. For everyone looks out for his own interests, not those of Jesus Christ. But you know that Timothy has proved himself, because as a son with his father he has served with me in the work of the gospel" (Phil. 2:20–22).

I had the privilege of hearing the late Dr. Henrietta Mears speak on a number of occasions. This great woman of God never married—but she had more "spiritual children" than most people. At one time it was said that she led more people to Jesus Christ on the West Coast than any other spiritual leader. One of her greatest thrills was to see hundreds of young men who attended her Bible classes go into the ministry. One of these young men was Bill Bright, founder of Campus Crusade for Christ, who still pays tribute to Dr. Mears for the impact she had on his life. And Billy Graham once wrote that no woman outside of his mother had more influence on him.

Personalizing these Principles

The following questions will help you apply these principles in your life. Read them prayerfully and answer them:

1. Have you experienced true freedom in Christ, both in your relationship with God and in your relationships with other Christians?

2. To what extent do you lack self-respect because you're not living a consistent Christian life?

   NOTE: When you answer this question, make sure you're evaluating your walk with God in the light of biblical guidelines and principles—not someone's legalistic standard. Legalism creates false guilt—which will certainly affect how you feel about yourself. Legalism keeps us in bondage. The teachings of the Word of God set us free.

3. To what extent are you allowing your need to be "approved by men" to override your desire to be "approved by God"?

4. Would you describe your relationship with Jesus Christ as a true friendship? If not, why not?

5. Children are truly a gift from God. However, do you have a "true son in the faith" that you've led to Christ and brought "up in the training and instruction of the Lord" (Eph. 6:4)?

Set a Goal

Review the five principles in this chapter and select one that you feel you need to give the most attention. For example, you may be living for the approval of men rather than the approval of God. Or, you may lack respect for yourself because you are deliberately violating the will of God. Whatever your particular need, set a personal goal:

_____

_____

_____

_____

Memorize the Following Scripture

I thank my God every time I remember you. In all my prayers for all of you, I always pray with joy because of your partnership in the gospel from the first day until now, being confident of this, that he who began a good work in you will carry it on to completion until the day of Christ Jesus.
                                                    PHILIPPIANS 1:3–6

Growing Together

The following questions are designed for small group discussion:

1. Can you identify with any of the specific ways God brought emotional healing to Joseph's life? Will you share with us that area of identification?

2. Since all of us experience emotional pain to one degree or another at various times in our lives, would you share one of those painful experiences?

3. How has God brought emotional healing in your life— or, are you still suffering from this pain? If so, would you feel free to share your experience with us to encourage us or so that we might encourage you?

4. How has your relationship with Jesus Christ brought emotional healing in your life?

5. What can we pray for you specifically?

Chapter 9

Forgiveness—The Ultimate Test
Read Genesis 42:1–28

*T*he week I was writing this chapter, the complex that houses the offices of our ministry were set ablaze by an arsonist. The person or persons responsible deposited accelerants in at least five locations—beginning in my office. I lost about forty Bibles I've collected and used over the years—beginning with the first Bible I purchased after I became a Christian nearly fifty years ago. Whoever committed this evil deed destroyed approximately fifty of our offices. All fifteen of our full-time pastors lost their personal libraries. The fire was set in the early hours of the morning, so fortunately no one was injured in the blaze.

Why, Lord!

One of the questions we ask the Lord at a time like this is "Why?" Why do bad things happen to good people? God understands this question and He doesn't mind our asking. The reality is we may not understand the answer for a long time. In fact, we may never understand the answer completely until we are with Him in eternity.

As I sat and reflected on Joseph's challenge to forgive his brothers for selling him as a slave into Egypt, I could not deny that somehow and in some way God was at work in all that had happened this particular week. He allowed it in order to achieve divine purposes—many of which are not yet clear in our minds.

One thing that *is* clear, however, is that God wants us to forgive those responsible. This does not mean that they should not be brought to justice. However, our responsibility is to forgive and to pray for our enemies—that for their sake and ours, justice will be done and that they might come to know the living God (Matt. 5:43–48; 6:14–15). After all, the Scriptures tell us "it is a dreadful thing to fall into the hands of the living God" in an unrepentant state (Heb. 10:31).

Forgiving Those Who Sin against Us

This is a great struggle—to forgive those who have wronged us, even though they have not acknowledged the wrong or asked for forgiveness. The Bible nowhere indicates that our willingness to forgive should be predicated on the fact that someone has asked forgiveness or has been properly disciplined.

Jesus Christ exemplified forgiveness—both in His teaching and with His life. He instructed us to love our enemies and to pray for those who persecute us (Matt. 5:44). And when He hung on a rugged cross, He cried out for those who so cruelly nailed Him there—"'Father, *forgive them,* for they do not know what they are doing'" (Luke 23:34).

The temptation to vindicate ourselves or to retaliate is normal, especially when we meet face to face with those who have offended and hurt us. At that moment, whether or not we have *truly* forgiven is put to the test. It's easier to *forget* the pain and hurt when we're separated physically. But when we interface, all the old mental and emotional memories tend to come to the surface. These scars are "psychological strawberries" that can easily be rubbed raw.

Joseph certainly faced the temptation to retaliate—to vindicate himself. His brothers had treated him cruelly. Though he was certainly not without fault (we never are), Joseph did not deserve such evil treatment. His emotional pain must have been almost unbearable.

But we've already seen Joseph's true character. He held no grudges. God had brought unusual healing to his heart and mind—enabling him to "forget" all of his trials in Egypt as well as what happened in Canaan. However, he was about to experience his greatest test!

Meanwhile, Back in Canaan

The "seven years of great abundance" had come and gone in Egypt and the "seven years of famine" had hit full force—not only in Egypt but in other countries. The land of Canaan was not exempt. Fortunately, Jacob had learned via the nomadic "internet" that there was "grain in Egypt" (42:2). His sons were evidently sitting around wringing their hands and "looking at each other." Jacob chided them for their irresponsible behavior and told them to go down to Egypt to buy food.

The famine that hit Canaan was serious. Jacob spelled that out when he told them to make this trip so that they might "live and not die" (42:2). Evidently, the land had not produced crops. Their sheep and goats and other animals—a part of their livelihood—would die first. And once that happened, it would only be a matter of time before sickness and death would take its toll on all who lived there.

Jacob took no chances regarding his youngest son. He sent the ten older brothers and kept Benjamin at home. The biblical statement says it all—"He was afraid that harm might come to him" (42:4).

Over twenty years after Joseph had supposedly been killed by a wild animal, Jacob was still hurting deeply over what he thought was Joseph's cruel death. He didn't want to lose the one that had taken Joseph's place in terms of affection and love.

Jacob's decision also indicates that he didn't trust the ten older brothers to protect Benjamin. Though he didn't blame his sons directly for "Joseph's death," he probably let them know often that Joseph was on a mission to discover how they were doing—to check on their welfare (37:14). Imagine the guilt these brothers must have felt all those years, knowing the truth but never revealing it to their father.

Face to Face

Ironically, God used this severe famine to bring the sons of Jacob face to face with their brother Joseph (42:5–8).

When they arrived in Egypt, they were ushered into his presence—not realizing that their brother was now governor of all Egypt. Imagine for a moment what Joseph must have felt when he looked up and saw ten men bowing low before him. He recognized them immediately (42:7). Though time had certainly taken its toll, he knew who they were. Their tan, weather-beaten faces were those of shepherds and their beards set them off from the clean-shaven Egyptian men.

Though Joseph recognized his brothers, he sensed they did not know who he was. After all, he was only seventeen when they last saw him—and now he was nearly forty. His hairstyle reflected the Egyptian culture and he stood before them in royal garb. It's understandable why they didn't know who he was. Furthermore, in their own minds he was probably dead—and dead men tell no tales! And if he weren't dead, they certainly did not anticipate meeting him in a governor's mansion.

Hiding all kinds of emotions that were churning inside him, Joseph quickly studied each brother carefully—counting as he took note of them. There stood Reuben, the oldest—the brother who had actually saved his life (37:21). Simeon, Levi, Judah, Issachar, and Zebulun—all sons of Leah—were present and accounted for. No doubt, standing together were Dan and Naphtali—sons of Bilhah, along with Dan and Asher, sons of Zilpah. But where was his youngest brother, Benjamin? The numbers didn't add up!

What were Joseph's thoughts and feelings at this moment? One thing for sure—they were certainly mixed. On the one

hand, he probably had an intense desire to reveal his identity—
to let them know he was alive and well. On the other hand, he
knew he might not get the answers to the questions that were
flooding his mind. What were their attitudes *now?* Had they
changed? Were their hearts soft and tender toward God? What
was their relationship with their father? Was Jacob even alive?
And what about his younger brother, Benjamin? Where was he?

Flashbacks

In a moment like this, the mind does strange things! Details of
events that happened years before are often condensed into an
instantaneous flashback (42:9). As Joseph watched his brothers
bow down before him, faces to the ground, he suddenly—but
silently—recounted in exact detail what had happened more
than twenty years before when his troubles actually began. He
remembered his own dreams that had created such intense
jealousy and hatred.

In his first dream, Joseph saw sheaves of grain. He was in
the field binding those sheaves and suddenly his sheaf "rose
and stood upright" and his brothers' sheaves gathered around
him and "bowed down to it" (37:7).

In Joseph's second dream, "the son and moon and eleven
stars" bowed down to him (37:9). In his naiveté, Joseph had
shared these dreams with his brothers and his father. Though
unaware of the prophetic and supernatural significance of
these dreams at that time, his brothers concluded very quickly
that Joseph was placing himself in authority over them
(37:10–11). They hated him for it. And when his father had
presented him with a richly ornamented robe, they were so
angry they plotted to kill him!

As Joseph witnessed his brothers bowing low before him,
he must have been overwhelmed with emotion. His dreams
had literally come true. At this moment—twenty-two years
later—what he had experienced in his mind was being fulfilled before his very eyes. His brothers *were* bowing down

before him. He *was* in a position of honor, power, and authority over them.

What an Opportunity to Retaliate!

What happened that day became a "master key" in unlocking his understanding regarding why God had allowed him to be sold into Egypt. Seeing God's purpose in it all must have helped dissipate any lingering anger he naturally would feel at that moment. He had every opportunity to retaliate. His brothers had no choice in the matter. He was in control and they were at his mercy.

Joseph had several options. He could have imprisoned them in order to let them experience how it feels to be incarcerated in a strange land with no one to represent your case. He could have sent them back to Canaan without food, which would lead to a slow but certain death. He also had the authority to accuse them of being spies and then have them executed.

Joseph chose the third option, but for one purpose—he needed to know the truth! Ultimately, he had their best interests at heart. He knew they weren't spies, but he didn't know whether or not they were telling him the truth about his father and his brother Benjamin.

"You Are Spies!"

Joseph did have legitimate concerns! After all, his brothers had acted wickedly on numerous occasions (37:2). Not only had they mistreated him, but they had little regard for the negative impact their actions would have on their aging father. And what about Benjamin? Had they treated him badly? After all, it would be natural for Jacob to focus his attention and affection on Joseph's little brother when he was told that his favorite son was killed by a wild animal. Did this create the same kind of jealousy and subsequent actions against Benjamin? Is that why he wasn't there? Was he even alive?

Tough Love

Joseph needed answers to these questions. Consequently, he chose to use a strategy that must have created intense pain for him personally (42:7–13). Forcing himself to control his emotions, he acted as if he didn't know them and "spoke harshly to them"— not to retaliate but to try to discover what had happened since he had last seen them. He wanted to know what was going on in their hearts. "'Where do you come from?' he asked, pretending 'to be a stranger'" (42:7).

Over the years, Joseph had become a very wise and shrewd man. He knew this basic question would open a door to more dialogue. Predictably, his brother's response was straightforward and to the point. They had come "to buy food" (42:7).

At that moment, Joseph must have forced himself to shout at them—"'You are spies! You have come to see where our land is unprotected'" (42:9). Painful as it was, Joseph knew he had to threaten them in order to get at the truth. And they knew his accusation meant that they could be imprisoned and executed!

Digging Deeper

Understandably, Joseph's brothers were shocked! Defending themselves, they repeated why they were there. But Joseph asked more pointed questions that are not recorded here—questions that his brothers later reported to their father. "'The man [referring to Joseph] questioned us closely about ourselves and our family. 'Is your father still living?' he asked us. 'Do you have another brother?'" (43:7).

Their answers to these questions must have set Joseph's heart pounding with relief. "'Your servants were twelve brothers, the sons of one man, who *lives* in the land of Canaan,'" they reported. "'The youngest is *now* with our father, and one is *no more*'" (42:13).

Jacob was alive! And so was Benjamin—*if* they were telling the truth. Joseph knew he needed to dig deeper into their souls.

What Was Really in Their Hearts?

What comes out of the mouth is not necessarily what's in the heart. Joseph needed more information before he could risk letting them know who he really was. More specifically, he wanted to check the truthfulness of their report about Benjamin. After all, they had lied to their father about Joseph. Could they be lying about Benjamin?

"'You are spies!'" Joseph repeated (42:14)—keeping the pressure on! But at the same time, he gave them a way out—telling them he would allow them to prove that they were being honest. "'You will not leave this place unless your youngest brother comes here'" (42:15). Joseph continued, spelling out his plan: "'Send one of your number to get your brother; the rest of you will be kept in prison, so that your words may be tested to see if you are telling the truth. If you are not, then as surely as Pharaoh lives, you are spies!'" (42:16).

Joseph put his brothers "in custody for three days" (42:17)—a very wise decision. He needed time to think. After all, his encounter with his brothers was intensely emotional. To complicate things, he couldn't express his true feelings. It's at times like this we need space—time to reflect and gain perspective.

Apparently, Joseph concluded that his original decision was too severe. Seeing only one son return while the others were imprisoned in Egypt may have been more than his father's old heart could handle. Furthermore, Jacob might not believe the report from only one brother. And practically speaking, Joseph knew that one man alone could not take enough grain back to Canaan to care for his father and his extended family.

During this three-day period, Joseph also had time to mentally process the answers his brothers had given during the interrogation. According to the biblical text, there was one very important omission. They had said nothing about God. What were their attitudes toward Him? Had they continued all these years to violate His commandments and will? Were their consciences still seared and hardened? Or had they softened their hearts and developed spiritually?

Sometime during this three-day period, Joseph changed his plan. He also decided to test their attitude toward God. To do so, he let them know that he—a high-ranking Egyptian official—believed and served the same God they worshiped.

Hard Hearts Are Softened

"'Do this and you will live, *for I fear God,*'" he said (42:18). Then, Joseph spelled out his new plan: "'If you are honest men [which was the real issue with Joseph], let one of your brothers stay here in prison, while the rest of you go and take grain back for your starving households. But you must bring your youngest brother to me, so that your words may be verified and that you may *not die*'" (42:19–20).

Guilt has a way of coming to the surface. For more than twenty years, Jacob's sons had tried to hide their sin. They may have even refused to talk about it, for fear Jacob would find out. But they had not forgotten their heinous crime. Though they were probably relieved that only one of them would have to stay in Egypt, they were under great conviction because of what they had done to Joseph. While preparing to leave, they discussed their predicament openly with each other, probably acknowledging their sin for the first time in twenty years.

Joseph's strategy worked, which is clear from the biblical account: "They said to one another, 'Surely we are being punished because of our brother. We saw how distressed he was when he pleaded with us for his life, but we would not listen; that's why this distress has come upon us.' Reuben replied, 'Didn't I tell you not to sin against the boy? But you wouldn't listen! Now we must give an accounting for his blood'" (42:21–22).

Listening In

Joseph's brothers didn't realize it, but he understood every word they were saying (42:23). Though he had become proficient in the Egyptian language, he never forgot his mother tongue. For the first time in his encounter with his brothers, he was beginning to get answers. They were all sorry for what they had done! And at this point, Joseph also learned that they thought he was dead—even though they had not killed him that awful day years ago. But they were now acknowledging that they were still responsible for "his blood" once they had sold him as a slave to the Midianite merchants.

When their hearts began to soften, we catch a glimpse of what was deep in Joseph's heart. He could no longer bear to stand and listen to their conversation and watch their painful expressions. His emotions began to erupt and before they could sense that this countenance was beginning to change, he left their presence and "began to weep." All the emotional pain he had experienced over the years blended with feelings of relief and probably even joy (42:24).

We don't know how long Joseph left his brothers' presence and cried tears of relief. However, we are told that he regained control of himself and determined that it was not yet time to reveal his identity. Though he was confident their hearts were beginning to change, he was not yet sure of their motives. It is one thing to admit guilt and "be sorry" when we're caught in our own web of sin. However, it's another thing to admit guilt because we're truly sorry for what we've done. At this point, Joseph wasn't certain which was which and he forced himself to stick to his original plan. He retained Simeon, even having him "bound before their eyes," (42:24) and then sent the other nine back to Canaan with their bags filled with grain.

Another Test

Unknown to his brothers, Joseph had given instructions to "put each man's silver back in his sack"—perhaps a symbol of what they had done to him when they sold him to the Midianite merchants "for twenty shekels of silver" (37:28). What would they do with this money? This was another test to determine if they were now being honest.

That night when they stopped to rest, one of Joseph's brothers discovered the money. The results were traumatic! When they all discovered the same thing happened to each of them, we read that "their hearts sank and they turned to each other trembling and said, 'What is this that *God* has done to us?'" (42:28).

As far as we know, this was the first time these men had acknowledged openly that God was involved in what was happening to them. At least to this point, the biblical record does not tell us that they even used His name. Though they talked about being "punished" because of what they had done to Joseph, they did not acknowledge the *source* of that punishment.

Joseph's brothers were sincerely frightened. How could they explain all of this to their father? Were they being forced to reveal all they had done to their brother Joseph? Would their father even allow them to take Benjamin to Egypt—especially if they told him what they had *really* done to Joseph?

Furthermore, what would happen if they did return to Egypt? How could they explain all of this to the Egyptian ruler? Obviously, they would be accused of stealing. Joseph's brothers found themselves in a serious dilemma—as most people do when they sin and try to cover it up. It may take years for the results of that sin to come to full fruition, but it will happen! And the longer we live in that situation with that sin unconfessed and in a state of unrepentance, the more complex and complicated the results. What we see happening to Joseph's brothers certainly and dramatically illustrates this reality.

Becoming God's Man Today

Principles to Live By

There are many principles that emerge from this story. But I must admit that the experiences I've gone through with our office fire surfaced several principles that apply more directly to my own situation. As you reflect on your own life experience at this moment, you may want to reword these principles or add to them.

Principle 1. When someone wrongs us, we're to forgive unconditionally even though that person may not admit it was wrong or ask forgiveness.

As of this writing, we don't know who started the fire in our offices, totally destroying everything except some records in our metal file cabinets. Most of us have lost personal items that can never be replaced. Our missions pastor lost mementos from all over the world—precious gifts that came from people in third world countries who had no way to give except some personal item from their own home.

I lost a beautiful metal sculpture of Moses reading the Ten Commandments—a gift created by one of the most renowned metal sculptors in all Brazil. This wonderful gift was given to me by a Christian brother I had ministered to in this country— a prized possession he had purchased for himself.

Should we forgive whoever did this terrible thing—even though we don't know who did it? "Yes," said Jesus. "'Love your enemies,'" He taught, "'and pray for those who persecute you'" (Matt. 5:44).

Before Joseph ever met his brothers when they came down to Egypt to buy food, he had forgiven them for what they had done to him. His life is a beautiful Old Testament illustration of what Jesus taught centuries later.

Principle 2. True forgiveness does not mean we will not continue to experience some negative emotions.

Many Christians get confused at this point. They forget that forgiveness is an act of the will. We can truly forgive and yet have negative feelings toward people who have hurt us—especially at certain moments in our lives.

As my wife and I rummaged through my office, using a shovel to see if anything had survived under the debris and piles of ashes, I could not help but have some negative feelings about the one who created this devastating loss. In fact, I shared with my wife I'd like to have this person in front of me in handcuffs and walk him or her through the rubble, asking some very pointed questions, such as, "Are you happy now? Does this make you feel good?" In essence, I was expressing that I'd like to "rub this person's nose" in this mess!

Does that mean that we've not forgiven this individual? Not at all! In fact, we've not only forgiven this individual but we've been praying for this person—that he or she might confess this terrible sin and come to know the Lord Jesus Christ as personal Lord and Savior.

Yes, we've forgiven this person, but as Christians we still have some negative feelings—and we'll probably have these feelings to a certain degree in days to come. And if we ever interface with this person, we'll have more negative feelings. The true test of our forgiveness is not if we have eliminated all negative feelings, but rather, whether or not we allow these negative feelings to keep us from doing what is right in spite of these feelings. In time, of course, these negative feelings will also dissipate and come into conformity with what we have already done as an act of the will.

Principle 3. Granting forgiveness and praying and hoping for justice are not incompatible concepts.

Following the fire, I asked our church body not only to forgive this person and to pray for him or her, but to also pray that this arsonist would be brought to justice. Our motive, I warned, must not be revenge. That's God's business. Paul wrote, "Do not repay anyone evil for evil. . . . Do not take revenge, my friends, but leave room for God's wrath, for it is written: 'It is mine to avenge; I will repay,' says the Lord" (Rom. 12:17, 19).

Ultimately, God will deal with this person—especially if he or she does not come to repentance. But God has also ordained that society be ruled by those who enforce laws and maintain order. In this sense, the Lord Himself has established the principles of justice. Therefore, it is our responsibility to cooperate fully with law enforcement officials and to pray that God will help them find this person and solicit a confession—not only to bring this person to justice, but to provide all of us with a sense of peace and security. Obviously, as long as an arsonist is at large, that person can strike again!

Joseph wanted justice and as prime minister of Egypt, he could make sure it happened. In his case, of course, he hoped that his brothers' hearts had changed—or would change! To achieve his goals, he used "tough love"—even threatening them with imprisonment and execution. Let me say it again. Loving, praying for, and forgiving our enemies and, at the same time, praying and hoping for justice are not incompatible principles in God's scheme of things.

Principle 4. When we have been wronged by someone who has not admitted it or sought forgiveness, we should have as our primary concern that person's relationship with God.

Joseph illustrates this principle beautifully. As we've already noted, he was very concerned about his brothers' relationship with God. Had they truly repented? Were they truly sorry because of their sin? Or, were they just sorry because they had gotten caught?

In the Book of Hebrews we read, "It is a dreadful thing to fall into the hands of the living God" (Heb. 10:31). This, of course, applies to anyone who has not confessed their sins and sought forgiveness. It applies particularly to those who are trying to destroy the work of God. This warning is directed also to Christians, for Paul wrote to the Corinthians and warned them because of their divisiveness. "Don't you know," he said, "that you yourselves are God's temple [the church] and that God's Spirit lives in you? If anyone destroys God's temple, God will destroy him; for God's temple is sacred, and you are that temple" (1 Cor. 3:16–17).

Here Paul was definitely referring to the "people" of God—the body of Christ. But this teaching certainly also applies to destroying anything that interferes with what God's people are doing to carry out His work.

Another Lesson from Corrie

I wish I could say that after a long and fruitful life, traveling the world, I had learned to forgive all my enemies. I wish I could say that merciful and charitable thoughts just naturally flowed from me and on to others. But they don't. If there is one thing I've learned since I've passed my eightieth birthday, it's that I can't store up good feelings and behavior—but only draw them fresh from God each day.

Maybe I'm glad it's that way, for every time I go to Him, He teaches me something else. I recall the time—and I was almost seventy—when some Christian friends whom I loved and trusted did something which hurt me. You would have thought that, having been able to forgive the guards in Ravensbruck, forgiving Christian friends would be child's play. It wasn't. For weeks I seethed inside. But at last I asked God again to work His miracle in me. And again it happened: first the cold-blooded decision, then the flood of joy and peace. I had forgiven my friends; I was restored to my Father.

Then, why was I suddenly awake in the middle of the night, rehashing the whole affair again? My friends! I thought. People I loved. If it had been strangers, I wouldn't have minded so.

I sat up and switched on the light. "Father, I thought it was all forgiven. Please help me do it."

But the next night I woke up again. They'd talked so sweetly too! Never a hint of what they were planning. "Father!" I cried in alarm. "Help me!"

Then it was that another secret of forgiveness became evident. It is not enough to simply say, "I forgive you." I must also begin to live it out. And in my case, that meant acting as though their sins, like mine, were buried in the depths of the deepest sea. If God could remember them no more—and He had said, "[Your] sins and iniquities will I remember no more" (Heb. 10:17)—then neither should I. And the reason the thoughts kept coming back to me was that I kept turning their sin over in my mind.

And so I discovered another of God's principles: We can trust God not only for our emotions but also for our thoughts. As I asked Him to renew my mind He also took away my thoughts.

He still had more to teach me, however, even from this single episode. Many years later, after I had passed my eightieth birthday, an American friend came to visit me in Holland. As we sat in my little apartment in Baarn he asked me about those people from long ago who had taken advantage of me.

"It is nothing," I said a little smugly. "It is all forgiven."

"By you, yes," he said. "But what about them? Have they accepted your forgiveness?"

"They say there is nothing to forgive! They deny it ever happened. No matter what they say, though, I can prove they were wrong." I went eagerly to my desk. "See, I have it in black and white! I saved all their letters and I can show you where. . . ."

"Corrie!" My friend slipped his arm through mine and gently closed the drawer. "Aren't you the one whose sins are at the bottom of the sea? Yet are the sins of your friends etched in black and white?"

For an astonishing moment I could not find my voice. "Lord Jesus," I whispered at last, "who takes all my sins away, forgive me for preserving all these years the evidence against others! Give me grace to burn all the blacks and whites as a sweet-smelling sacrifice to Your glory."

I did not go to sleep that night until I had gone through my desk and pulled out those letters—curling now with age— and fed them all into my little coal-burning grate. As the flames leaped and glowed, so did my heart. "Forgive us our trespasses,"

Jesus taught us to pray, "as we forgive those who trespass against us." In the ashes of those letters I was seeing yet another facet of His mercy. What more He would teach me about forgiveness in the days ahead I didn't know, but tonight's was good news enough.

Forgiveness is the key which unlocks the door of resentment and the handcuffs of hatred. It breaks the chains of bitterness and the shackles of selfishness. The forgiveness of Jesus not only takes away our sins, it makes them as if they had never been.[1]

Personalizing These Principles

Reflect on these four principles as well as Corrie ten Boom's experience. Isolate those principles you may be violating. The following questions will also help you:

1. Have you truly forgiven those who have wronged you?

2. Are you confused because you still have negative feelings toward someone—even though you believe you have forgiven them?

3. Have you been able to truly forgive and yet pray that justice might be done, and, at the same time, have right motives?

4. Is your primary concern for those who have sinned against you that they might develop a right relationship with God by confessing their sins?

Set a Goal

As you've evaluated your own life in the light of these principles from Joseph's experience, select a principle or principles you've violated the most and set a personal goal. Perhaps, like Corrie ten Boom, you're harboring evidence with the primary motive of vindicating yourself or taking vengeance. If so, set a personal goal to change both your attitudes and actions:

_____

_____

_____

_____

Memorize the Following Scripture

Therefore, as God's chosen people, holy and dearly loved, clothe yourselves with compassion, kindness, humility, gentleness and patience. Bear with each other and forgive whatever grievances you may have against one another. Forgive as the Lord forgave you.
Colossians 3:12–13

Growing Together

The following questions are designed for small group discussion:

1. How do you handle forgiveness, particularly when it comes to forgiving someone who has sinned against you and has not admitted it or sought forgiveness?

2. How do you handle negative feelings that tend to surface, even though you have forgiven someone as an act of the will?

3. What additional principles can we glean from Joseph's life in relation to forgiveness?

4. Is there any experience you'd feel free to share where you are presently struggling with forgiving someone who has hurt you?

5. How can we pray for you particularly?

Chapter 10

Rebuilding Trust
Read Genesis 42:29–44:34

*T*rust is one of the most significant ingredients in all human relationships. Without it, marriages blow apart, families disintegrate, churches split, friends are alienated from each other, and businesses fail. Trust *can* be rebuilt, but usually not without a lot of hard work combined with God's supernatural intervention in the hearts of everyone involved.

Joseph's relationship with his brothers is a classic case of what it takes to rebuild trust. What makes this story so helpful and encouraging is that trust was reestablished in spite of deep hurt caused by jealousy, hatred, and the worst kind of dishonesty and deception.

To be able to once again trust his brothers, Joseph needed to know and believe two things—that they were telling him the whole truth, and that they were truly sorry for what they had done, both before God and man.

Even if his brothers were telling the truth, had they experienced a change of mind? What was their motivation? What was in their hearts? Were they remorseful because they were in trouble or because they had sinned against God and members of their family? Down deep, were they still controlled by jealousy? Were they still insensitive toward their father's feelings? And were their consciences still hardened toward God and His righteous laws? Before Joseph felt free to reveal who he really was, he had to have answers to these questions.

A Detailed Report

When Joseph's brothers returned to Canaan, they shared everything that had happened in Egypt—that they had been treated harshly and accused of being spies (42:30). They told Jacob how they had tried to convince the Egyptian ruler that they were "honest men" with only one objective—to buy food in order to live (42:31).

With heads hung low, they also reported that this powerful man would not believe them until he had visible evidence. He wanted to see for himself if they really had a younger brother named Benjamin. If they refused to bring this "living proof," they could not "trade in the land" (42:34). To be more specific, they had been threatened with starvation!

To add to what they knew had already upset their father terribly, they also opened their sacks of grain and showed Jacob the silver that had been returned. We read that "when they and their father saw the money pouches, they were *frightened*" (42:35). The Hebrew word translated "frightened" is *Yare,* which describes intense negative emotions. We can only imagine the incredible fear and despair that must have gripped their hearts at this moment in their lives!

Understandably, Jacob was devastated! Pointing an accusing finger at his sons, he poured out his deep feelings of sadness— "'You have deprived me of my children. Joseph is no more and Simeon is no more, and now you want to take Benjamin. Everything is against me!'" (42:36). Chuck Swindoll describes this response as "the groanings of a sad dad"!

Reuben's Panic Attack

Jacob's despair impacted Reuben, Leah's firstborn and the oldest son (42:37). Foreseeing a deadlock, he panicked, becoming almost irrational. "'You may put both of my sons to death if I do not bring him back to you. Entrust him to my care,'" Reuben pleaded, "'and I will bring him back'" (42:37).

Jacob would never have taken the life of his two grandsons—no matter what happened. But Reuben's response demonstrates the deep frustration and anxiety he felt—not only because of what *was* happening but what *had* happened! He had felt distrust from his father for years. Jacob probably told him many times that he would never entrust one of his sons to him again because of what happened to Joseph.

Remember, too, that Reuben still felt the sting of his father's disappointment because of the way in which he betrayed Jacob's trust by defiling his bed. The Scriptures report that he "went in and slept with his father's concubine Bilhah"—the mother of his two brothers, Dan and Naphtali (35:22). Though we're not told how Jacob handled the situation at the time, we do know—as we noted earlier—that he never forgot what Reuben had done, even to his dying day. This is clear from his final words to his oldest son years later after they had all moved to Egypt. What Jacob said then is a clue as to how he felt throughout the years: "'Reuben, you are my firstborn, my might, the first sign of my strength, excelling in honor, excelling in power. Turbulent as the waters, you will no longer excel, for you went up onto your father's bed, onto my couch and defiled it'" (49:3–4).

This lack of trust certainly weighed heavily on Reuben. Regarding Joseph, he probably felt his father's disappointment in him was unfair—making himself a victim. After all, he was the one who had "tried to rescue" Joseph "from their hands." He had planned to remove his brother from the cistern and "take him back to his father" (37:21–22). But his lips had been sealed all these years! He had become part of a deceptive plot and there was no way he could communicate with his father his initial intentions without exposing his brothers—and himself! Consequently, being the oldest, he had to bear final responsibility for Joseph's welfare in spite of his efforts to save him.

Reuben's offer to allow Jacob to take the lives of his two sons if he did not prove trustworthy was a desperate effort to regain his father's trust and his position in the family. But once again, it didn't work! Once again, he felt that deep rejection when Jacob wouldn't budge. "'My son will not go down there with you,'" Jacob responded. "'His brother is dead and he is the only one left. If harm comes to him on the journey you are taking, you will bring my gray head down to the grave in sorrow'" (42:38).

What happened to Reuben is a pathetic and tragic reminder that in some situations we can make mistakes that take us beyond the point of no return in certain human relationships. There seems to be no way to rebuild trust, no matter what our efforts. Thank God, those are rare circumstances. But Reuben's experience is a solemn warning to us all!

Judah's Rational Stance

Jacob's negative response to Reuben's emotional plea seems to have ended the discussion—but only temporarily (43:1–10). The devastating effects of the famine didn't allow the matter to lie dormant. Jacob himself brought up the subject again when their supply of grain was depleted. "'Go back and buy us a little more food,'" he said (43:2).

This time Judah, the fourth oldest son, stepped forward. Perhaps standing eye to eye, he reminded his father of what they had already reported—that they wouldn't even get an audience with the Egyptian ruler if they did not return with Benjamin. Judah's response was pointed and firm—"'If you will not send him, *we will not go down*'" (43:5)!

At this point, Jacob chastised his sons for revealing the fact that they even had a younger brother (43:6). But their response was straightforward and accurate. If they were to be honest, they had no choice! The questions were too specific: "They replied, 'The man questioned us closely about ourselves and our family. "Is your father still living?" he asked us. "Do you have another brother?" We simply answered his questions. How were we to know he would say, "bring your brother down here"?'" (43:7).

Since Reuben had lost the battle with Jacob, Judah knew that he had to take charge of the situation if they were to survive. Communicating much more rationally than Reuben, Judah told Jacob that he would personally "bear the blame" the rest of his life if he did not bring Benjamin back safely (43:9).

Jacob's Reluctant Concession

After what appears to have been a rather intense argument, Jacob finally consented. He saw he had no choice if they were to survive the famine. Trying to make the best of a terrible situation, Jacob instructed his sons to take some gifts to the Egyptian ruler and to take enough money to pay back what was returned in their sacks of grain as well as enough to pay for a new supply. Though deeply distressed and bereaved that he had to make this horrendous decision, Jacob hoped against hope that God would bring them all back safely (43:11–14).

Unexpected Welcome

When Jacob's sons arrived in Egypt, to their surprise, they were taken to Joseph's private mansion (43:15–25). Predictably, they were gripped with fear, thinking they were going to be charged with stealing the silver they had found in their sacks and then taken captive as slaves.

These men wasted no time seeking out Joseph's steward—the man who had handled the transaction initially—and hurriedly explained what happened. Nervously, they showed him the money they brought back.

This was a wiser move on their part than they realized! Unknowingly, they had used the opportunity Joseph gave them to demonstrate honesty—the very aspect of their lives that was in serious question.

Imagine their surprise—and relief—when the steward told them not to worry. He remembered having received their silver. And imagine, too, what must have gone through their minds when he said, "'Your God, the God of your father, has given you treasure in your sacks'" (43:23).

An Amazing Response!

At this moment, Jacob's sons must have looked at each other in amazement! Here was a polytheistic Egyptian talking about their God and the God of their father. The name of God had probably been mentioned more frequently by the Egyptians than it had been by them over the past twenty years. After all, when we're in violation of God's commands and will and weighed down with guilt—as Joseph's brothers were—we usually don't want to talk about spiritual issues. Personally, I don't even like praying! In reality, I'm trying to ignore God! Has that ever happened to you?

An Emotional Moment

When Joseph arrived home, his brothers had already laid out their gifts (43:26). Though grateful, Joseph quickly zeroed in on his greatest concern. "'How is your aged father you told me about? Is he still living?'" (43:27).

Even though Joseph had changed his plan to keep only one of the brothers in Egypt, he no doubt spent some sleepless nights wondering if his father's old heart could handle the strain of having to send Benjamin to Egypt. Imagine the relief Joseph felt when they responded that their father was "still alive and well" (43:28).

This was the moment Joseph had been waiting for. Hardly able to contain his emotions, he once more surveyed the scene before him. His eyes quickly fell on the youngest—a twenty-three-year-old—perhaps a spitting image of himself when he was Benjamin's age. There was no way he could have recognized Benjamin except by his features that reflected that they both had the same father and mother. The last time Joseph had seen him, Benjamin was only a toddling one-year-old.

"'Is this your youngest brother, the one you told me about?'" Joseph asked, trying to control his emotions. Wanting to throw his arms around his younger brother, Joseph restrained himself and somehow uttered the words, "God be gracious to you, my son'" (43:29).

Meeting Benjamin after those many years of separation was too much for Joseph. He could not maintain his emotional control. He was "deeply moved at the sight of his brother" (43:30). But Joseph also maintained sufficient rational control to know that this was not yet the time to reveal his identity. He quickly turned, "hurried out" and "went into his private room and wept there" (43:30).

Joseph finally regained control of himself. When he was certain they couldn't see the redness in his eyes, he returned and to his brothers' astonishment, he had his servants seat his brothers chronologically—"from the firstborn to the youngest." How did he know their ages? Imagine the look in their eyes when Joseph had Benjamin served "five times as much as anyone else's" (43:33–34).

It was not unusual for a high official to serve larger portions to a person who occupied a place of honor. But it was a privilege reserved for a prince or ruler. For example, the Spartans *doubled* the portions, and the Cretans served *four times* the usual amount. It's clear Joseph wanted to make a point when he served Benjamin *five times* more than any of his other brothers.[1]

Were There Any Signs of Jealousy?

Joseph was deeply concerned about his brothers' jealous attitudes and behavior that had erupted more than twenty years ago resulting in such intense hatred that they wanted to take his life. Had they changed? Or had they simply transferred that hatred to Benjamin?

Think about how intently Joseph must have studied their faces and their overall body language while Benjamin was being treated so royally. He must also have strained his ears to pick up bits and pieces of communication that must have gone on among his brothers while all of this was happening. We're not told what he saw or heard, but he must have been pleased.

But Joseph was still not satisfied that he had the answers

to his final question. How could he be sure they had really changed? He could not see it in their hearts. He felt he had to take one more step.

A Final Test

When Joseph's brothers were ready to leave for Canaan, Joseph instructed his steward to give them as much food as they could carry, but to once again return their money, and to put his own personal silver cup in Benjamin's sack. After they were well on their way, Joseph then sent his steward after them to accuse them of stealing (44:1–14).

Predictably, Joseph's brothers were aghast! They were so certain of their innocence, they offered the life of the one who had done such a thing (44:9). They quickly opened their sacks to prove they were not guilty. But to their astonishment, there was Joseph's silver cup in Benjamin's sack! They were so frustrated and distraught that they literally "tore their clothes" (44:13).

Joseph had thought through this strategy carefully. He had instructed his chief steward to tell his brothers *before* he conducted his investigation that whoever had the cup would become a slave and the rest were free to go (44:10). If they had been jealous of Benjamin when he was treated so royally at the banquet, they may have been able to mask their feelings. But they could not hide their true feelings now!

There was no question in Joseph's mind what they would have done years ago. More specifically, if Judah had responded as he did when they decided to sell Joseph into Egyptian slavery, he would have taken the lead in seeing that Benjamin bear the blame and become the slave. What this would do to Jacob would not have been even a consideration. But their reactions this time were different—much different. All of them— together—returned to Egypt to face this criminal charge!

Imagine Joseph's relief and joy when he saw them with their little parade of donkeys entering the palace gates. They were a pathetic sight with heads bowed low, their garments torn, and their long flowing hair and full beards matted because of the mixture of dust and tears that flowed from their eyes. But to Joseph, they were now men who were more concerned about their aged father and their younger brother than they were about themselves. They had passed the test! They had changed from the inside out!

The Finishing Touch

Judah passed the test even more nobly than the others (44:15–34). When they were ushered into Joseph's house, he stepped forward. He made no excuses, uttered no rationalizations, and made no attempts to cover up their sinful actions that spanned the twenty-two-year period. "'What can we say?'" he said. "'How can we prove our innocence?'" And he then uttered his most repentant statement to date—"'God has uncovered your servants' guilt'" (44:16).

With this confession, Judah was acknowledging their sin against Joseph. Though he did not mention Joseph's name, it's easy to read between the lines. But more important to Joseph was Judah's statement, "'We are now my lord's slaves—we ourselves and the one who was found to have the cup'" (44:16).

Judah made it clear they would not forsake Benjamin. If he became a slave, they would all become slaves. Though innocent of the charge of stealing, Judah was acknowledging that they were guilty of a much greater sin—a sin God had uncovered.

The fact that Judah acknowledged that God Himself had uncovered their sin is significant. Since they believed Joseph was dead, they were acknowledging God's sovereign intervention. Unknown to them, of course, Joseph was involved as an instrument for righteousness in the hand of God. Furthermore, the fact that they did not feel pressured into this confession by Joseph verifies the wisdom their brother exemplified in choosing to remain anonymous.

As Joseph listened to Judah's confession, he must have yearned to enfold Judah in his arms and weep with joy. Yet he restrained himself. He had one more question in his mind that was yet unanswered. How did Judah—and his older brothers—actually feel about Jacob at this moment? What concern did they have for their aged father? Consequently, Joseph responded to Judah's confession by telling him that "only the man who was found to have the cup" would become his slave. "'The rest of you *go back to your father in peace*'" (44:17).

Judah's response must have overwhelmed Joseph! Judah focused his thoughts and feelings on Jacob. He reviewed their father's response when they had returned from Egypt to Canaan the first time: "'If the boy is not with us when I go back to your servant my father and if my father, whose life is closely bound up with the boy's life, sees that the boy isn't there, *he will die.* Your servants will bring the gray head of our father down to the grave in sorrow'" (44:30–31).

After demonstrating great concern for their father, Judah then took the final step in his confession. He pleaded with Joseph to set Benjamin and his other brothers free and he would personally take his little brother's place as a slave. "'How can I go back to my father if the boy is not with me?'" he asked. He then answered his own question, "'No! Do not let me see the misery that would come upon my father'" (44:34).

Joseph now had the answer to his final question—and more! Here stood the man who had convinced his brothers to sell him as a slave to a band of Midianites now offering to be a slave in Benjamin's place. Here stood the man who years ago could have cared less about the impact Joseph's death would have on his father. But now he was so concerned about Jacob that he was willing to remain in Egypt so Benjamin could return. *This was true repentance!*

The Shock of a Lifetime!

Hearing Judah's final statement, Joseph could contain himself no longer (45:1–3). He had everyone ushered from the room except his brothers. There he revealed his true identity, weeping and wailing so loudly he could be heard even beyond the confines of his mansion. Judah's confession had unraveled his soul.

Joseph's brothers were totally caught off guard. They had no clue whatsoever that the man who had tested them so severely was their own brother. They were so shocked and terrified that they could not utter a word and, initially, could not accept it as a reality. But what happened that day in that room is in itself another story—to be continued in the next chapter. For now, let's look carefully at what these events teach us about rebuilding trust.

Becoming God's Man Today

Principles to Live By

Why didn't God simply reveal to Joseph in a dream what was in his brothers' hearts? Why did he have to resort to using human wisdom to determine whether or not they were honest? Obviously, God wanted Joseph, his brothers, and his father to go through this painful but healing process—a process leading them to true repentance—normally an experience God has chosen not to supernaturally circumvent when it comes to our spiritual growth.

Principle 1. *Trust is a precious commodity, and we must do all we can to maintain it.*

It takes years to develop trust. However, we can quickly destroy it with self-centered actions. Sadly, only one major sinful action can destroy that trust—particularly when it involves an act of immorality. And when trust is gone, we've lost one of our greatest assets.

Fortunately, not all of our actions are that serious. In fact, we can rebuild trust by being honest and open. Most people—even non-Christians—are very forgiving when this happens.

Think for a moment about Richard Nixon when he had to resign as President of the United States because of his involvement in Watergate. What would have happened had he gone before the American public and confessed this sin and asked forgiveness—explaining openly and honestly what happened? My personal opinion is that the American people would have forgiven Mr. Nixon. But because he tried to cover up his sin, he lost the battle and his greatest commodity—trust. There is a lesson here for all of us which leads to our next principle.

Principle 2. If we do something that violates trust, we should try to rebuild it with total honesty and true repentance.

I've known men who have committed adultery. When they've been discovered, predictably their wives have several basic questions. How long has this been going on? Has it happened with other women? How many times has this happened?

Sadly, some of the men have not been honest. Their wives discover later that what they were told was a "one night stand" had happened again and again! Obviously, this does not build trust. Rather, it destroys what remnants of trust there may have been left in the relationship.

I remember one day talking with a well-known pastor who had been caught in immorality. According to his report, it involved two women. Later, it was discovered that it involved many more—which was reported openly in a sophisticated Dallas publication. What this pastor was attempting to rebuild was utterly destroyed with his dishonesty.

I know another man who was also caught in adultery. When confronted, he admitted his sin and wept openly, seeking forgiveness from his wife and from his fellow Christians. His sorrow seemed so real that everyone forgave him—but he was not truly repentant. Rather, he was "sorry" he had gotten caught. Later, he resorted to dishonesty and continued his involvement with the "other woman." What trust he had regained with his "sorrowful act" was once again destroyed— this time more so!

Trust *can* be rebuilt—but it will take honesty and openness and a true change of heart and mind—which means a change in behavior. One very important way to demonstrate honesty and true repentance is to submit to an accountability system on a regular basis. This involves meeting with one or more mature men to answer some specific questions regarding daily activities and behaviors.

Principle 3. If we cannot rebuild trust as we would like, we must not make ourselves the victim but rather go forward in our lives and develop our relationship with Christ.

I remember talking one day with a man who had made some very foolish decisions. As a result, other Christians were affected and were trying to resolve some of the problems this man had created. As we talked, it became obvious that this man was angry at those who had become involved in the situation.

At this point, I asked this man who had caused the problem in the first place. He had to admit that he did. I then pointed out to him that he was making himself the victim and accusing others of being the perpetrators.

As a pastor, how often I've seen this happen! It's a human tendency. When a person's sin hurts others who in turn try to correct the problem, those who are trying to help are often accused of inappropriate involvement. How tragic! This, of course, is also a sign of dishonesty—more often than not, self-deception. It is also an indication there has not been true repentance.

Principle 4. If our trust has been violated, we must do all we can to help that person rebuild that trust.

This is the true test of our own maturity—and whether or not we have truly forgiven others for what they've done. I do not believe Jacob did what he could have to help Reuben rebuild trust. On the other hand, Joseph stands out as a shining and noble example. In spite of their terrible sin against him, he did all he could to help his brothers rebuild their relationship with him—not by simply accepting their statements of being honest but by helping them go through a process leading to true repentance. This leads us to another important principle.

Principle 5. It's always wise to test a person's honesty and trust, but it must always be done with proper motives and appropriate methods.

Joseph clearly demonstrates that it's not wrong to test others in order to determine whether or not they are being honest and truly repentant. However, at this point, we must be careful not to act out of revenge or anger. Our motives must be based on a desire to restore a person and to help rebuild trust.

Obviously, this is very difficult, especially if we happen to be the person who has been hurt. We'll probably need help from other mature Christians to help us test our own motives. Are we being driven by anger? Are we attempting to hurt the person and get even?

Don't misunderstand! "Tough love" involves "tough decisions." Again, Joseph demonstrated this reality. But inside—in his heart—Joseph was doing what he knew needed to be done in spite of his desire to reveal his identity immediately. He was doing what was best for his brothers.

Because this is a very difficult process, Paul established a very important principle in his letter to the Galatians. Note his instructions: "Brothers, if someone is caught in a sin, you who are spiritual should restore him gently. But watch yourself, or you also may be tempted. Carry each other's burdens, and in this way you will fulfill the law of Christ" (Gal. 6:1–2).

Paul made it clear in this passage that it normally takes *more than one person* to help restore the one who has sinned against us or someone else. This is why he used the plural pronoun "you."

Notice that Paul also said, *"You who are spiritual."* This means that if we've been the one who has been sinned against, we must look at our own hearts. We must be in fellowship with God. Furthermore, those who help us must also be in proper fellowship with God.

But there is another very important guideline. This whole process must be done with *gentleness* and *true humility*. In the process, we must realize that we might become guilty of the very same sin. This is why it's important to check our own motives and utilize methods that are appropriate to the situation.

Personalizing These Principles

The following questions will help you apply these principles to your own life:

1. Am I doing anything in my life that might lead to a violation of trust?

2. Are there any areas in my life where I feel I have violated someone's trust? If so, have I made an effort to rebuild trust with total honesty and true repentance?

3. Have I done something to violate the trust others have placed in me but am now blaming others for doing things that have resulted from my own sinful actions?

4. If someone has violated my trust, what am I doing to help that person rebuild that trust?

5. If I am trying to help a person rebuild trust, what am I doing to test that person's honesty and trust? Furthermore, what are my motives in testing whether or not this person is sincere? Are the methods I'm using to test this person's sincerity appropriate to the action and reflective of my own proper relationship with God?

Set a Goal

Review the principles for rebuilding trust. The above questions will help you isolate a principle or principles you need to apply right now. For example, you may have violated someone's trust but have made no open and honest effort to repair the damage. Set a personal goal to apply this particular principle or other principles:

_____

_____

_____

_____

Memorize the Following Scripture

Brothers, when someone is caught in a sin, you who are spiritual should restore him gently. But watch yourself, or you also may be tempted. Carry each other's burdens, and in this way you will fulfill the law of Christ.

GALATIANS 6:1–2

Growing Together

The following questions are designed for small group discussion:

1. As a group of Christian men, what steps can we take to make sure that we maintain trust?

2. Would you feel free to share a personal experience where you have violated trust but have now rebuilt that trust? Would you feel free to share the process you went through?

3. Have you ever been tempted to make yourself a victim when you have been the cause of the problem? Why is this so easy to do?

4. Can you think of someone who has violated your trust? What steps could you take to help that person rebuild that trust?

5. What methods have you used to test whether or not a person is being honest and truly repentant? How did you determine that your own motives were right when you put this person to the test?

Chapter 11

Big Boys Do Cry!
Read Genesis 45:1–24

*H*ave you ever heard someone say, "Big boys don't cry"? One Sunday morning, I asked the men in my congregation how many had heard that statement as a child. I then asked the same basic question of the women, but changed the word "boys" to "girls." The difference was startling! Men everywhere shot up their hands, while a much smaller number of women responded. This difference is why many of us as men today can't cry. We've been programmed to believe what we've been taught. Actually, we've been sent an emotionally damaging message—mostly in the early years of our lives. You see, big boys *do* cry—strong men who are growing and maturing both emotionally and spiritually—and Joseph's life story proves it!

When Judah reached the final step in his repentant confession, actually pleading that he be allowed to take Benjamin's place as a slave, Joseph "could no longer control himself" (45:1). The powerful urge to reveal his identity—which had almost taken over on several previous occasions—now overwhelmed him. He knew this was the time to tell them who he was. His questions were all answered. His brothers had told the truth. He believed that both Benjamin and his father were still alive.

More importantly, their hearts had changed. They did not—and would not—treat Benjamin like they had treated him more than twenty years earlier. Neither would they lie to Jacob. Rather, they were deeply concerned about his physical and emotional well-being. And most of all, Joseph's brothers had acknowledged their sin against God, followed by a deep and sincere repentance.

"Have Everyone Leave My Presence!"

All this time Joseph had revealed very little emotion to his brothers. They had only observed him as a stern, rational, and cold-hearted Egyptian ruler. And at times when he could not mask his feelings, he had left the room to weep in private. You can imagine what his brothers must have thought when they saw their accuser begin to lose emotional control and heard him cry out, "'Have everyone leave my presence!'" (45:1).

At this moment, Joseph's brothers were on trial! Benjamin had been accused of stealing Joseph's silver cup. Judah was pleading for mercy. When they saw Joseph's outburst, they could only conclude that the "axe was about to fall!" They would naturally think that they had made this Egyptian official so angry that he was either going to imprison them for life or sentence them to death! There was no way they could have interpreted Joseph's reactions as positive. They must have recoiled from this emotional outburst with intense fear.

Joseph wept and wailed "so loudly" that the Egyptian attendants he had ordered to leave the room could still hear what was happening (45:2). Without question, they would have quickly passed the word onto Pharaoh, perhaps reporting that their master had just gone insane—possibly crumbling psychologically from the heavy task of directing the gigantic storehouse operation and the distribution of grain (45:2).

There are normally two reasons for this kind of deep sobbing. Either we are feeling deep sorrow and emotional pain or we're experiencing psychological release. Often, these reasons overlap.

I remember one time in my own life when I wept so uncontrollably it almost scared me. I actually cried out from the depths of my soul. I experienced an unbelievable crisis in the ministry. My personal pain was very intense but generally I managed to keep my emotions under control. But when I saw what this experience was doing to my family, I could bear it no longer. I wept uncontrollably with sobs that came from deep within me.

I'm confident Joseph wept this way many times during his own experience in Egypt after he had been betrayed by his brothers. But at this moment in his life—when he decided to let his brothers know who he really was—his motivation for weeping was much different. He was experiencing deep emotional release! He no longer needed to test his brothers to see if they were being honest. He knew they were different. Joseph's capacity to weep over what was happening at this moment would actually put the finishing touches on whatever healing he still needed. His tears were those of relief and joy—not pain and suffering. His wailing only indicated how difficult it had been to hide his true feelings and to put his brothers through such a difficult period of testing.

We're not told how long Joseph wept uncontrollably, but anyone who has experienced this kind of emotional release knows that it takes time. One thing is sure. The ordeal lasted long enough for word to get back to "Pharaoh's household" (45:2).

"I Am Joseph!"

When Joseph finally gained emotional control, he identified himself. "'I am Joseph!'" (45:3)

Joseph's next question takes us even deeper into his heart. "'Is my father still living?'" he asked. Though he had believed Judah's report, his question now was more rhetorical—revealing how much he had missed Jacob. Though he had believed intellectually, he was having difficulty believing emotionally. It was as if it were too good to be true!

Remember, also, that Joseph had taken a serious risk over the last several months by testing his brothers so intensely. His greatest fear in his attempt to get at the truth was that if indeed Jacob was still alive, he might have pushed him over the edge, causing such trauma that his father's old heart might have stopped beating. What a surge of relief to get this reassuring word that his father was still alive! This, too, contributed to his deep emotional release.

When Joseph's brothers heard him identify himself by name, they were so stunned and overwhelmed with fear they couldn't utter a word. We read that "they were *terrified* at his presence" (45:3). They couldn't believe what they were hearing and seeing. After all, they had repeatedly told the story that Joseph was dead! And even though they knew he had not been mauled to death by a wild animal, they had long since concluded that he had been slain in Egypt.

At that moment, their unbelieving hearts must have been flashing questions on the "screens" of their minds. How would this Egyptian ruler know about Joseph? Though they had alluded to him, there is no evidence they had even used his name. They had simply identified him as the "one" who was "no more" (42:13).

Perhaps they thought this was proof positive that this Egyptian ruler was clairvoyant. This thought must have gone through their minds ever since he had seated them "in the order of their ages, from the firstborn to the youngest" (43:33). Furthermore, the Egyptian ruler's servant had just accused Benjamin of stealing his master's silver cup which he used "for divination" (44:5).

It would be easy for them to conclude at this moment that this was the ultimate in God's judgment for what they had done to their brother Joseph. In their minds, God may have been using a pagan Egyptian ruler to reveal their sins against Joseph—actually enabling him to call their brother by name. Or, could this have actually been their brother's spirit talking to them through another human being?

Obviously, none of these conclusions were true! Joseph wasn't clairvoyant, though on several occasions God had supernaturally revealed the future to him through dreams. He hadn't resorted to divination—incantations and ceremonies used by pagan soothsayers. The servant's reference to the mysterious use of the "silver cup" was no doubt part of Joseph's plan to test his brothers' sincerity. This man who had identified himself as "Joseph" was Joseph!

"Come Close to Me"

Joseph could readily see the unbelief and fear in their eyes. Though he was speaking their language perfectly—which probably frightened them even more—Joseph's appearance was Egyptian. He knew he had to help them accept the fact that he was indeed their brother. That's when he asked them to "come close" to him (45:4).

What happened at this moment? Was Joseph simply asking them to draw near so he could look deep into their eyes, saying, "'I *am* your brother, Joseph, the one you sold into Egypt'" (45:4)?

I think something happened that is not described. We must remember that God had confirmed His promise to Abraham hundreds of years earlier with a unique sign—the rite of circumcision. This was not a mark of shame or embarrassment. This was a symbol of God's unconditional covenant with Abraham, Isaac, Jacob, and all the sons of Israel (17:9–14). All young boys were to be circumcised. From God's perspective, this was serious business, for He said to Abraham, "'Any uncircumcised male, who has not been circumcised in the flesh, will be cut off from his people; he has broken my covenant'" (17:14).

Some Bible expositors believe that in that private and intimate setting, Joseph revealed to them that he was like them. He, too, was circumcised—a mark of a true son of Abraham and something that set all of them apart from their pagan neighbors. No Egyptian man had that unique distinction. In fact, to be like a Hebrew would be a disgrace. Remember that for Egyptians to even "eat with Hebrews" was "detestable"! (43:32).

At that moment, Joseph also revealed to his brothers they were all children of the covenant and that is ultimately why God in His sovereign purpose sent him to Egypt—"to preserve . . . a remnant on earth . . . by a great deliverance" (45:7). God was keeping His promise to Abraham, Isaac, and to their father, Jacob.

"Do Not Be Distressed"

Whatever transpired in that intimate moment, Joseph's brothers now believed they were face to face with the one they had sold into Egypt many years before. Predictably, their fear and anxiety suddenly turned to distress and self-hatred. Shame must have consumed them. How could they look into their brother's eyes? How could they have been so evil? Their feelings of remorse, regret, and guilt must have been overwhelming!

Joseph's true character shines at this moment! He quickly attempted to put them at ease—to dissipate their intense feelings of guilt. He wanted them to know that he had not tested them to make them suffer but rather to discover the truth—and he didn't want them to suffer now. "'Do not be distressed'" he pleaded. "'Do not be angry with yourselves for selling me here.'"

Joseph's next statement must have overwhelmed them even more—not with fear but with a sense of awe: "'It was to save lives that God sent me ahead of you. . . . God sent me ahead of you to preserve for you a remnant on earth and to save your lives by a great deliverance'" (45:5–7).

"God Sent Me Here"

Joseph's next statement was magnanimous, extremely sensitive, and designed to help his brothers overcome the shame they were feeling. "'So then,'" he reassured them, "'it was not you who sent me here, but God'" (45:8). They had suffered enough. He did not want them to continue to blame themselves. Though they had committed a horrible sin, Joseph wanted them to see that God had an ultimate purpose in allowing all of this to happen (45:8–15).

We're not told at what point in time Joseph gained this clear spiritual perspective on why he had to suffer. Perhaps it first began to come into focus when he saw his brothers bowing before him and remembered the dreams of his youth. Even at that moment, he may have begun to strategize for their future welfare—especially for his father. It would not be surprising that he began immediately to plan to bring them to Egypt in order to protect them and to provide for them.

However, Joseph could not carry out his plan without knowing his brothers' spiritual condition. He could not move forward without knowing for sure how they felt about Jacob—and Benjamin. How they felt about them would be how they still felt about him.

There was no logical way Joseph could justify his desire and plan to Pharaoh if their hearts had not changed. It would only create havoc and disunity in his royal court—and eventually in all Egypt. It would threaten the very position God had called him to fulfill. And if they had not changed in their hearts, Pharaoh would have never had compassion on Joseph's brothers. We can now see that this was probably another reason why Joseph had to know the truth! He would never be able to gain Pharaoh's ultimate blessing on his plan if he were not convinced in his own heart that his brothers had changed.

Don't misunderstand! Joseph had sufficient authority to decide for himself that he could bring his family to Egypt. Pharaoh would never question his decision. In fact, Joseph made that decision before consulting Pharaoh. He informed them that the Lord had made him "father to Pharaoh, lord of his entire household and ruler of all Egypt" (45:8). Joseph could do what he felt was best—and he did. He told them to waste no time going back to Canaan, reporting to Jacob what had happened and then issuing a personal invitation to return to Egypt. And before he even consulted Pharaoh, Joseph obviously had already decided where he wanted Jacob's extended family to live—in the region of Goshen—one of the most fruitful and productive areas in all of Egypt.

Before his brothers departed Egypt to carry out Joseph's instructions, we see one of the most tender and beautiful scenes in all of Scripture. Joseph "threw his arms around his brother Benjamin and wept, and Benjamin embraced him, weeping." He then "kissed all his brothers and wept over them" (45:14–15). And once they had been totally reunited in heart and spirit, they sat together and talked—obviously experiencing deep fellowship and communion. Ironically, this was probably something they had never done before. This is a beautiful picture of what God wants to happen among all of His children within the family of God!

"I Will Give You the Best of the Land"

When Pharaoh heard all that had happened, he "and all his officials were pleased"—which verifies the extent to which everyone in Pharaoh's court trusted Joseph (45:16–20). In fact, Pharaoh not only approved Joseph's overall plan, but added some specifics of his own. "'Bring your father and your families back to me,'" he said. "'I will give you the best of the land of Egypt and you can enjoy the fat of the land'" (45:18). Pharaoh instructed them further not to bring any of their personal belongings because he would provide them with all new things—"The best of all Egypt" (45:20).

This is another beautiful picture of what happens when people confess their sins to God and accept His forgiveness in Jesus Christ. We shed our spotted and sinful robes and are clothed in His righteousness (Gal. 3:27).

This was probably the first time, in a long time, Pharaoh had told Joseph what to do. And he hurriedly carried out the king's orders. His emotions must have been bubbling over with joy. Though he knew he had the authority to make this kind of decision, think how wonderful it made Joseph feel to have Pharaoh's approval, his total cooperation, and active participation. I'm confident this is what he had hoped and prayed for all along. And now it was happening! Imagine what Pharaoh was thinking. If these men were anything like Joseph, he saw them all as assets to his kingdom rather than liabilities. How ironic!

"Don't Quarrel on the Way!"

With Pharaoh's blessing and approval, Joseph carried out his orders (45:21–24). Note that he gave Benjamin "three hundred shekels of silver and five sets of clothes." Ironically, his brothers had sold him to the Midianite merchants for *eight ounces* of silver. At this moment, Joseph rewarded Benjamin with *eight pounds!* But what made this such a joyous moment is that there doesn't appear to be any jealousy—only rejoicing that they could return Benjamin to their aged father with five beautiful sets of clothes. Years earlier, they had returned from the fields with a single torn garment spotted with blood!

After loading the carts, giving his brothers new clothes as well, and providing them with provision for the journey, Joseph sent them on their way. But his parting words are classic and were probably uttered with "tongue in cheek." With a twinkle in his eyes and a smile on his face, he must have teased them as they left the palace grounds saying, "'Don't quarrel on the way!' (45:24).

I'm confident Joseph's brothers responded with an approving laugh and their own "thumbs up" way of signaling to Joseph that they had gotten the message! This was a true sign of a restored relationship and that all had been forgiven. When we can laugh at our mistakes and feel at ease with ourselves, we've come a long way on our journey toward maturity!

A Perspective on Joseph's Tears

We know more about Joseph's tears and why he wept than any other Old Testament character. We've already noted four specific occasions that he wept—all associated with his brothers' trip to Egypt. We'll observe three more before we conclude this study. These seven events, of course, do not include the numerous times he must have cried himself to sleep after he had been so ruthlessly separated from his father and sold as a slave at the tender age of seventeen.

What we know of Joseph's tears reflect, not just his humanness, but his heart attitude. Here was a man who had more power, prestige, and authority than any man in the world. And yet he never lost his ability to be tender, to show compassion, and to feel deeply. He was definitely a man's man—but a *gentle* man! He certainly demonstrated that "big boys do cry"!

Softened Hearts

➤ Joseph wept when he saw his brothers' hearts begin to soften in their relationship to God (42:21–24).

The first time the Holy Spirit pulls a curtain on Joseph's heart and lets us peer deep into his soul involved the intense conversation his brothers were having in his presence. They did not realize their brother could understand what they were saying. Joseph had just informed them that one of them would be detained and put in custody while the others returned to Canaan to get Benjamin. "'Surely,'" they said to one another, "'we are being punished because of our brother. We saw how distressed he was when he pleaded with us for his life, but we would not listen'" (42:21).

Reuben then reminded them of his own warning at that time: "'Did I not tell you to not sin against the boy? But you wouldn't listen! Now we must give an accounting for his blood'" (42:22).

As Joseph listened in on this conversation, he could not control his emotions. We read that "he turned away from them and *began to weep*" (42:24).

What prompted Joseph to shed tears at this time? Certainly the conversation brought back some very painful memories. He remembered his own cries for mercy and how they turned their backs on him and wouldn't listen. But more importantly, Joseph cried because he was emotionally touched when he heard them begin to acknowledge their sin.

Benjamin's Welfare

➤ Joseph wept out of compassion when he learned that his brother Benjamin had not suffered the same plight he had suffered (43:30–31).

The second time we're told that Joseph cried is when he first encountered Benjamin after his brothers returned from Canaan. He was "deeply moved at the sight of his brother"— so much so that he "hurried out and *looked for a place to weep.*" Eventually he ended up in his private room where he obviously shed more tears of relief (43:30).

For years, Joseph had wondered how his brothers had been treating Benjamin, envisioning the possibility that they'd actually done the same thing to his little brother that they had done to him. In his heart, Joseph was rejoicing because Benjamin had not suffered as Joseph had suffered.

True Repentance

➤ Joseph wept because he saw Judah's true concern for his father, Jacob (44:33–45:2).

As we've noted in this particular study, Judah's repentant confession and his sincere request that he be allowed to take Benjamin's place as a slave so that their father would not suffer any more emotional pain touched Joseph more than any event. He wept uncontrollably because he saw true repentance— particularly in Judah's heart. Here stood the man that had made the suggestion that he be sold into slavery twenty-three years ago, now willing to become a slave himself so that their old father would not suffer as he had suffered before.

Reconciliation

➤ Joseph wept when he was reconciled with his brothers (45:14–15).

The fourth instance where Joseph wept is perhaps the most touching scene thus far. As we've seen, it happened after Joseph revealed his identity and when his brothers really understood who he was and that he held no grudges. Joseph "threw his arms around his brother Benjamin and *wept,* and Benjamin embraced him, *weeping.*" And then, what probably was a first in their family experience, Joseph "kissed all his brothers and wept over them" (45:14–15). These were definitely tears of rejoicing because of the reconciliation that had taken place.

Reunited

➤ Joseph wept when he was reunited with his father (46:29).

When Jacob finally arrived in Egypt, we read that Joseph "threw his arms around his father and *wept for a long time*"

(46:29). What an incredible reunion! More than anything, Joseph had definitely missed his father's love and affection. Being reunited brought great rejoicing to his heart.

Jacob's Death

> ➤ Joseph wept when his father died (50:1).

Death is probably one of the most common reasons for weeping in every culture in the world. This happened seventeen years after Jacob arrived in Egypt with his family (47:28). We read that "Joseph threw himself upon his father and *wept over him* and kissed him" (50:1).

I remember when my own father died. I hadn't seen him for a couple of years—which I regret. But when I walked into the room where he lay in a casket, my eyes filled with tears. I reached out and touched his hand, realizing emotionally for the first time that he wasn't just asleep. In fact, Dad was not even there. I only touched the "house" he had lived in for seventy-eight years. He was with the Lord—and though I wept tears of grief, they were not only tears of sorrow but tears of rejoicing knowing my dad was "away from the body and at home with the Lord" (2 Cor. 5:8; Phil. 1:23–24).

Compassion

> ➤ Joseph wept when he saw the grief caused by his brothers' lingering guilt (50:17).

After Joseph's father died, his brothers were afraid that he might seek revenge. Consequently, they sent a message to their brother that their father requested of Joseph before he died that he forgive them for their wrongdoing. We read that "when their message came to him, *Joseph wept*" (50:17). Perhaps more than any other event where Joseph cried, this instance reveals Joseph's heart of compassion. He had already forgiven them and it grieved him that they were still suffering from guilt and fear.

Becoming God's Man Today

Principles to Live By

Principle 1. God created all of us with the capacity to weep, and if we cannot under certain circumstances, it is not physically, psychologically, and spiritually healthy.

Weeping is a God-created means for emotional release. Research demonstrates that when people lose loved ones in death and do not allow themselves to weep at some point in time, they are probably headed for some future emotional struggles. In some instances, it may result in psychological depression or anger and bitterness. Let's not forget that when Jesus arrived in Bethany following the death of Lazarus, a very dear friend, He "wept" (John 11:35). The Son of God modeled for all of us that it's alright to cry.

Principle 2. Weeping can be a sign of great strength—not weakness.

No one who has a correct view of Joseph would ever classify him as being weak. He endured the most hurtful and painful of all experiences—rejection by his brothers—and yet he emerged stronger than ever. He did not allow bitterness to consume his being or to interfere with his ability to think clearly and to act responsibly.

Joseph then rose to a position of great prominence in Egypt. In the process, he did not allow rejection and anger nor human temptation to drive him to an illegitimate sexual relationship when the opportunity more than presented itself. Nor did he ever use his position of power to retaliate. We see in Joseph a man of great emotional and spiritual strength— though he often wept.

I remember a big strong football player who walked into our church one day. He used to be a quarterback for Southern Methodist University. His name was "Rusty" Russell. He'd just come into a personal relationship with Jesus Christ. He used to sit in church listening to the Word of God and to people sharing what Christ meant to them. Almost every Sunday following his conversion to Christ, big tears would fill his eyes and often flow down his cheeks. One day he said to a friend of mine, "You know, before I became a Christian I never cried—not once. Now I cry almost every Sunday!"

As men, we must not allow pride to keep us from doing what God says is normal. When we hurt, we must not be afraid to weep. The facts are that it may be our weaknesses that are keeping us from expressing our emotions in this way.

Principle 3. Though weeping is normal under certain circumstances, it should never be used as a means of manipulating others or used for selfish reasons.

It is no secret that some people develop the "art of weeping." I've seen preachers do it. I've seen musicians do it. If you've listened to them often enough, you can predict when it's going to happen. Furthermore, since weeping is more natural for women in our culture, it's very easy for them to develop the art of weeping in order to manipulate.

Isn't it amazing that everything that God has created to be good, human beings have a tendency to use selfishly and inappropriately. As we've noted, weeping is a very normal means of expressing emotion but we can also use it with false motives. When we do, we not only hurt ourselves, but we confuse others. Eventually, people will not take us seriously if we "cry wolf" too often.

Principle 4. Sincere weeping often clears the way for objective and honest communication with those who have hurt and wounded us.

We've already noted that after Joseph wept with his brothers, they spent time talking (45:15). This was probably the first time in their lifetime that Joseph and his brothers were able to sit down and have a time of mature and open communication. Weeping definitely set the stage for this kind of openness.

The same is true for most of us. Sincere weeping enables us to communicate with each other more effectively. The emotional layers are peeled back so we can be more objective and authentic. Furthermore, we can relate at a less serious level, even laughing at ourselves and our weaknesses. This seems to have happened when Joseph told his brothers not to quarrel on their way back to Canaan (45:24). It hardly seems logical that Joseph would be seriously admonishing them at this juncture. Rather, all of them seemed to be able to look at the mistakes and sins of the past and even inject some humor. This is often the true test of reconciliation—particularly when deep pain has broken human relationships.

Personalizing These Principles

Review the reasons Joseph wept and the principles that we can learn from this experience. Then, stop and think for a moment. Ask yourself the following questions:

1. When was the last time you wept?

   If you have not cried for a long time, perhaps (but not necessarily) you're bottling up and overly suppressing your emotions.

2. Why have you wept?

   To help you answer this question, check any of the following. If you can identify with any of Joseph's reasons for weeping, you can be sure you have cried for some very noble reasons.

   I've wept

   ❑ because I've seen people respond spiritually.

   ❑ because someone I love has been spared suffering.

   ❑ because I've seen someone deeply concerned for someone else.

   ❑ because I've been truly reconciled with someone who has mistreated me.

   ❑ because I've been reunited with a loved one or dear friend.

❑ because of the death of a loved one or close friend.

❑ because I've grieved over another person's lingering emotional pain.

Set a Goal

As you've reviewed Joseph's experience and attempted to personalize these principles from his life, set a personal goal!

_____

_____

_____

_____

Memorize the Following Scripture

There is a time for everything, and a season for every activity under heaven:
A time to weep and a time to laugh,
A time to mourn and a time to dance.
ECCLESIASTES 3:1, 4

Growing Together

The following questions are designed for small group discussion:

1. How has hearing the statement "Big boys don't cry" affected you?

2. How do you feel when you break down and cry in front of people?

3. When was the last time you cried? What prompted your tears?

4. Would you feel free to share why you have difficulty crying?

5. What can we pray for you specifically?

Chapter 12

Seeing Purpose in Suffering
Read Genesis 45:25–50:26

Several years ago, I stood in the kitchen at home talking with my oldest daughter. At that time, she was a teenager and struggling deeply with the problem of suffering in the world. Why would God allow it? Why do innocent people experience pain? Tears filled her eyes as she shared her heart. Frankly, I couldn't answer all of her questions, and as I held her close to me, I cried with her—sharing as honestly as I could that I, too, still had some of the same unanswered questions. But I also shared that I believed that God was just and fair and someday we'd understand.

All human beings struggle with the issue of "why bad things happen to good people." Ultimately, only God knows the answer to this question. But in the meantime, as we live our lives day by day we can be sure that "in all things God works for the good of those who love him" (Rom. 8:28). We may not understand it all, but we can learn a valuable lesson from Joseph who trusted God for years—not understanding what the purpose was in his own suffering. Eventually he understood—and so will we—if not on earth, in eternity.

"Jacob Was Stunned"

When Joseph's brothers returned from Egypt and told their aged father that Joseph was still alive, "he did not believe them." He "was stunned" (45:26)! After all of those years of thinking that Joseph had been torn to pieces by a wild animal, Jacob could not respond with hope. The memory of his son's blood-stained ornamented robe must have flashed through his mind—as it had a thousand times over the twenty-two-year period.

Evidence That Demands a Verdict

The more Jacob's sons talked and shared what Joseph had said, "and when he saw the carts Joseph had sent to carry him back," his spirit revived (45:27). It had to be true. There was too much evidence. Jacob must have sensed a new sincerity in his sons. They were different men. Furthermore, where would they have gotten so many things—their new clothing and the twenty donkeys—just for him—"loaded with grain and bread" (45:23)?

Seeing his beloved son, Benjamin, would be the most convincing evidence! There he stood, verifying his brothers' story—wearing brand new clothes with four additional sets in his arms. Imagine Jacob's emotional response when Benjamin unloaded his bags of silver—three hundred shekels in all—which was fifteen times the amount exchanged between the Midianites and Joseph's brothers when Joseph was sold into Egypt.

"'I'm convinced!'" Jacob cried out. "'My son Joseph is still alive. I will go and see him before I die'" (45:28).

Divine Confirmation

As soon as Jacob and his sons could get everything organized, they left for Egypt. On the way, they stopped in Beersheba where Jacob "offered sacrifices" to God (46:1). It was there the Lord also spoke directly to Jacob and affirmed what his sons had reported. The Lord also assured Jacob of His personal presence as he traveled to Egypt (46:2–4).

Stopping in Beersheba is significant! It was here that Jacob's grandfather, Abraham, and his father, Isaac, had lived years before. It was here that Abraham had "planted a tamarisk tree" and had also "called upon the name of the LORD" (21:33). It was in Beersheba that Abraham had died—still believing the promise that God would make him "into a great nation" (12:2). And it was here that God once again revealed Himself—this time to Jacob—reassuring him that the promise to Abraham would be fulfilled through him. Thus we read, "'I am God, the God of your father,' he said. 'Do not be afraid to go down to Egypt, for *I will make you into a great nation there.* I will go down to Egypt with you, and I will surely bring you back again. And Joseph's own hand will close your eyes'" (46:3–4).

Imagine Jacob's elation when God told him that "Joseph's own hand" would close his eyes when he died (46:4). Though Jacob had accepted the fact that Joseph was still alive, the Lord's affirmation was proof positive that he would see his beloved son again!

A Grand Reunion

Joseph had been anxiously waiting for his dad's arrival. And what a reunion it was! He traveled to Goshen and met his father there. When he saw Jacob, he "threw his arms around his father and wept for a long time" (46:29).

When Jacob finally gained enough emotional control to speak coherently, he uttered, "'Now I am ready to die, since I have seen for myself that you are still alive'" (46:30). It's difficult to imagine the scene. There they stood, arm in arm weeping and rejoicing at the same time.

Jacob's revived spirit did marvelous things to his old body—even at age 130. I'm reminded of the proverbs that state that "a cheerful heart is *good medicine"* (Prov. 17:22) and "pleasant words are a honeycomb, *sweet to the soul* and *healing to the bones"* (16:24). He lived another seventeen years and did not die until age 147 (Gen. 47:28). How much he must have enjoyed that period of time—which equaled exactly the time he had spent with Joseph before his son was sold into Egypt.

Jacob also spent these years in luxury, living in a section of Egypt unsurpassed in productivity. As Pharaoh promised, Jacob and his sons and their families could settle in the "best of the land of Egypt" where they could "enjoy the fat of the land" (45:18).

Jacob also basked in the unexpected pleasure of having fellowship with Joseph's children. What a delightful surprise to this old man who firmly believed he would never see Joseph again—let alone the thought of seeing Joseph's children. Shortly before Jacob died—while blessing Joseph's sons, Manasseh and Ephraim—he stated, "'I never expected to see your face again, and now God has allowed me to see your children too'" (48:11).

It's Time to Die

Just before Jacob died, he instructed that his body be taken back to Canaan so he could be buried in the same place as his grandfather, Abraham, and his father, Isaac (49:29–32). Interestingly, this was also where Jacob had buried his wife Leah (49:31). Could it be that Jacob felt remorse in his later years regarding the way he had treated Leah—showing unquestionable favoritism to Rachel. The biblical record is very clear that Jacob "loved Rachel more than Leah" (29:30).

After settling in Egypt and reflecting over the years, perhaps Jacob realized how much Leah had suffered—that she had not planned this clandestine marriage, but rather, had become a victim of her father Laban's wicked behavior. Furthermore, Leah had also born six of his sons—half of the men who became the foundation stones in building the great nation that God had promised!

It's also possible Jacob came to grips with what showing favoritism does within a family unit. Though God overruled the result of his wrongdoing, it was sin nevertheless—and his whole family paid a terrible price.

At Home with the Lord

Whatever Jacob's motivation for selecting this particular burial site, we read that when he "had finished giving instructions to his sons, he drew his feet up into the bed, breathed his last and was *gathered to his people*" (49:33). To quote the apostle Paul who wrote centuries later, Jacob was "away from the body and home with the Lord" (2 Cor. 5:8). Here is an Old Testament illustration that God is indeed the God "of the living," not "the God of the dead"—an argument Jesus used to convince the Sadducees that there is indeed a resurrection of the dead (Mark 12:27). The moment Jacob died, he "was gathered to his people." This is why Jesus told the Sadducees that the Lord was "the God of Abraham, the God of Isaac, and the God of Jacob" (12:26). What point was Jesus making at that moment? Jacob was very much alive and having fellowship with his father and his grandfather.

When Jacob died, we once again see Joseph's deep love for his father. He "threw himself upon" him "and wept over him and kissed him" (Gen. 50:1). For Joseph, this was not a mere formality—an expected cultural response when someone dies. This was true grief mingled with joy that he had been able to spend, not only his first seventeen years with his father, but the last seventeen years of his father's life.

A Royal Funeral

When Pharaoh heard about Jacob's desire to be buried in Canaan, he granted Joseph permission to honor his father's final request. In fact, the king treated Jacob as if he were Egyptian royalty (50:4–14). Pharaoh had all of his officials accompany Joseph, including "the dignitaries of his court and all the dignitaries of Egypt" (50:7). He also sent along "chariots and horsemen"— all in all "a very large company" (50:9).

What a tremendous parade of people this must have been! What pomp and circumstance! Think how Joseph must have felt. Seeing his father honored this way would have helped make his past problems and pain worth it all.

By honoring Jacob in this way, Pharaoh was honoring Joseph as well. It was Joseph's faithfulness to the king and his reputation in Egypt that caused Pharaoh to bestow such royal treatment upon Jacob.

What a sight it must have been when they finally laid Jacob's body to rest! Even the Canaanites recognized the magnitude of this royal burial! For seven days, Jacob's family went through the formality of mourning a departed loved one. Even the Egyptians participated in this solemn event (50:10–11).

A Nagging Question

Joseph was certainly rejoicing in Pharaoh's thoughtfulness and feeling a deep sense of gratitude as everyone traveled back to Canaan to bury his father (50:15–26). On the other hand, his brothers were deeply troubled. After Jacob died, fear began to well up in their hearts. A nagging question kept going through their minds: "'What if Joseph holds a grudge against us and pays us back for all the wrongs we did to him?'" (50:15).

Guilt has a way of lingering even though we are forgiven. This happened to the sons of Jacob. They knew Joseph's deep love for their father and that he would have done nothing to send the old man to an early grave. Though Joseph has assured them, both with his words and actions, that he had no animosity in his heart toward them, they were overcome with feelings of paranoia.

To understand this kind of fear, we need to be aware of how easy it is for people who have mistreated others to interpret another person's actions in light of their own weakness. How could Joseph forgive them for what they had done? From their own human perspective, they could not accept the fact that anyone could overlook such grievous ill-treatment without retaliating! His reactions couldn't be sincere. He must have been feigning forgiveness to protect Jacob. Joseph's acts of unselfishness in bringing them all to Egypt and bestowing upon them such rich blessings must have been to honor their father—to make up for all the heartache Jacob endured the past twenty-two years!

Why would Joseph's brothers think this way? The answer is really very simple. They could not have demonstrated the same attitudes and actions themselves. Consequently, they projected on Joseph their own weaknesses. Now that Jacob was gone, they braced themselves for the worst!

The Wisdom of This World

Throughout this ordeal, Jacob's sons had learned one important lesson—not to wait around for "the axe to fall"! Using what we might call the "wisdom of this world," they plotted a two-fold strategy to appease Joseph (50:16–18). Since they feared that Joseph's love and respect for Jacob may have been the reason he had not retaliated, they used that very love and respect as a basis of intercession. They sent word to Joseph that their father had left instructions before he died requesting that he forgive his brothers "the sins and the wrongs they committed" against him (50:17).

It appears this was a story they had fabricated out of fear. Joseph probably discerned what they were doing very quickly— which helps explain his own response. When he received their message, he once again revealed what was truly in his heart. He had forgiven them long ago, even before they initially came to Egypt. He had never planned to retaliate, even before they acknowledged their sins. At this moment, he was deeply touched by his brothers' anxiety and fear. He could not hold back the tears. He did not want them to continue punishing themselves because of what they had done (50:17).

Once their "father's message" had gotten through to Joseph, his brothers quickly followed this message with a personal appearance before Joseph. Again they "threw themselves down before him" and said, "'We are your slaves'" (50:18). This was a very sincere effort on their part to placate Joseph should he still be harboring a grudge. They were offering to serve him the rest of their lives if he would not imprison them or have them executed.

Interestingly, Joseph had not treated them as slaves the last seventeen years. Rather, he had treated them more like royalty. Why then would they be so fearful at this moment? In addition to believing that Joseph may have treated them this way because of their father, the very fact that Joseph had done so much for them probably accentuated their guilt!

In actuality, they had not come to understand "grace." Some Christians face the same problem when they learn that God forgives our sins—not because of any works we've done, but because of our confession and repentance. This is why some believers go through life trying to compensate for their sins, rather than accepting God's forgiveness as a free gift—an act of grace.

A Divine Perspective

Joseph responded to his brothers' fear both with a human as well as a divine perspective. On the one hand, he was sensitive to their fears and anxieties. He knew they were human and identified with their anguish. "'Don't be afraid,'" he said (50:19).

Joseph was reiterating what he had said the day he had revealed his identity seventeen years earlier. At that time, he told them not to "be distressed" or "angry at themselves." And once again, "he reassured them and spoke kindly to them" (50:21). He could not and would not retaliate.

"Am I in the Place of God?"

Joseph quickly reiterated why he would never retaliate. He was not that kind of man. He did not harbor bitterness. But even more basic than his gentle spirit and compassionate heart was the fact that his theology affected his attitudes and actions. Joseph understood God's perspective regarding what had happened. He made this divine point of view very clear when he asked his brothers a revealing rhetorical question: "'Am I in the place of God?'" (50:19).

Joseph was also modeling what Paul wrote hundreds of years later. "Do not repay anyone evil for evil" (Rom. 12:17). "Do not take revenge, my friends, but leave room for God's wrath" (12:19). Joseph was probably tempted to use his position of power to deliberately get even, but his divine perspective and God's love and power in his life enabled him to overcome that temptation.

In All Things

Joseph had come to see God's hand in all that had happened to him. Though there were times during that period in Egypt when he had to trust God in the midst of total darkness and total confusion, he now understood why he was sold into Egypt.

Joseph had stated that reason to his brothers the day he revealed his identity (45:5–8). But he knew he must reiterate it once again with even greater emphasis—and added insight and wisdom. Seventeen years before he made no reference to the evil part they played in it all. The focus was on God's sovereign plan for his life as well as theirs. "'It was to save lives that God sent me ahead of you,'" he had said (45:5). Elaborating, he continued—"'God sent me ahead of you to preserve for you a remnant on earth and to save your lives by a great deliverance. So then, it was not you who sent me here, but God'" (45:7–8).

Dealing with Sin

On the human side, Joseph's brothers had sinned terribly when they sold him into Egypt as a slave. They had also sinned exceedingly when they lied to their father and put him through such terrible suffering. At this moment, Joseph sensed that his divine perspective on what happened was not enough to deal with their sin. His brothers needed to hear him acknowledge that what they had done was indeed wrong. And so he did! He informed them that he knew that they had "intended to harm" him. But he also blended this human perspective with his heavenly Father's perspective. Thus, he told them that even though they had sinned against him, "God intended it for good" (50:20). Though neither Joseph nor his brothers could ever fully understand this kind of paradoxical thinking, this expanded explanation put the finishing touch on their restored relationships. As far as we know, these men not only accepted God's forgiveness but forgave themselves.

"Here Lies Joseph, a Man of Character!"

Joseph had this divine perspective on what had happened to him until the day he died. Though he was considerably younger than most of them, God took him home before his brothers passed off the scene. Perhaps this happened in God's divine plan to give Joseph one more opportunity to demonstrate love and concern for his brothers before he joined his father, Jacob, his grandfather, Isaac, and his great-grandfather, Abraham. Knowing he was about to depart this life, he called his brothers together one day and said, "'I am about to die. But God will surely come to your aid and take you up out of this land to the land he promised . . . to Abraham, Isaac and Jacob.' And Joseph made the sons of Israel swear an oath and said, 'God will surely come to your aid, and then you must carry my bones up from this place'" (50:24–25).

Joseph then "died at the age of a hundred and ten." As "they embalmed him" and as "he was placed in a coffin in Egypt" (50:26), they laid to rest an Old Testament great who exemplified in a marvelous way what it means to be a man of character—a man who lived for God with all his heart in the good times as well as the bad. He is indeed a great model—and an example to us all!

Becoming God's Man Today

Principles to Live By

Principle 1. When God accomplishes divine purposes in spite of our sins, we must never excuse ourselves for doing what was wrong.

God is sovereign in all aspects of life. This was Joseph's perspective. Consequently, there are some who could read the story of his life and be tempted to blame God for their sin. After all, even though his brothers had committed a horrible crime, God used it to achieve His divine purposes. Doesn't this put the responsibility back on God?

James warned against this kind of thinking when he wrote, "When tempted, no one should say, 'God is tempting me.' For God cannot be tempted by evil, nor does he tempt anyone; but each one is tempted when, by his own evil desire, he is dragged away and enticed. Then, after desire has conceived, it gives birth to sin; and sin, when it is full-grown, gives birth to death" (Jas. 1:13–15).

Jacob's sons were responsible for their sins against Joseph and their father, even though God took their evil deeds and used them to accomplish His purposes. God did not cause these men to sin, but He used the results of their sin to accomplish His divine will and decrees. Only God can understand this antinomy. No human logic can explain it. But it's true nevertheless!

Principle 2. While on this earth, it's not possible to explain all human suffering.

Not all human problems and pain can be explained with Joseph's experience. God had a special plan for Joseph in allowing his suffering. Also, we know the end of the story! In God's scheme of things, he allowed Joseph to be able to see a specific purpose in what happened to him. There are times, however, that Christians suffer and we may never be able to explain why. For example, how do we explain rape to a person who has been marred for life? How do we explain child abuse that leaves an individual an emotional cripple? How do we explain mental torture that drives a person insane? How do we rationalize the ravages of war that leave thousands of people maimed for life?

Suffering in general is related to the fact that the world is contaminated by sin and there are two dimensions to this problem. First, we can use our freedom to sin and make innocent people suffer. Second, we can use our freedom to sin and cause severe suffering in our own lives. More often than not, both dimensions are interrelated.

Adolf Hitler is an example of the first dimension. Under his leadership, millions of innocent people experienced excruciating suffering—often leading to a horrible death. No one would conclude that God directed Hitler to do what he did. He did what he did because he had a free will and a sinful nature—and he deliberately used this freedom to hurt others and make them suffer. Consequently, God will hold Adolf Hitler responsible for his sins. I shutter to think of what this man and all of his henchmen will face at the judgment of God!

Principle 3. Though suffering can be difficult to explain and the reason for it may not be clear, a Christian has the potential to see meaning that others may not see.

Following are some of the specific purposes God can accomplish in and through our lives when we suffer:

1. We may have opportunities to communicate the gospel of Jesus Christ.

   When Paul was in prison in Rome, he wrote to the Philippians and told them that what was happening to him really served to "advance the gospel" (Phil. 1:12). This has also been true in the lives of many Christians who have suffered persecution over the years. They have turned it into an opportunity to witness for Jesus Christ.

2. Personal suffering can help us understand the sufferings of others.

   Paul also clearly illustrated this purpose in his second letter to the Corinthians: "Praise be to the God and Father of our Lord Jesus Christ, the Father of compassion and the God of all comfort, who comforts us in all our troubles, so that we can comfort those in any trouble with the comfort we ourselves have received from God" (2 Cor. 1:3–4).

On numerous occasions when I've been counseling those who have experienced unusual suffering through no particular fault of their own, I've often pointed out that God can use them in a special way to minister to others who are going through the same distress. No one can understand a rape victim like a person who has been raped. No one can appreciate the bitterness and the anxiety that is caused in a child's life because of divorce like a person who has gone through that particular trauma. No one can comprehend child abuse like a person who has gone through the experience. God can use these negative experiences to be a helpful influence in other people's lives who have suffered the same unfortunate situations.

3. Suffering can produce Christian maturity.

   James wrote that Christians should "consider it pure joy" when they "face trials of many kinds." He then states the reason—"Because you know that the testing of your faith develops perseverance. Perseverance must finish its work so that you may be mature and complete, not lacking anything" (Jas. 1:2–4).

   We must not define James' use of the word *joy* as "happiness" or "pleasure." Rather, it's a deep settled peace in the midst of pain that enables us to endure this kind of affliction, knowing we're in God's permissive will.

4. Suffering can bring an individual to a salvation experience.

   Suffering has been the occasion for some individuals inviting Jesus Christ to be their Savior. Without coming to the place of helplessness, they may never turn to God for help. In this sense, it's better to suffer in this life than spend all of eternity separated from God!

Principle 4. When we are able to see some meaning in our suffering, it gives us inner strength to endure in ways that are beyond our normal human capacities.

This is a universal principle, which is dramatically illustrated by Dr. Victor Frankl when he was taken prisoner by the Nazis and confined to a concentration camp. Frankl was a Jewish psychiatrist. Because he was in good health, rather than being ushered off to the gas chambers, he had to work long hours in the field.

People working alongside Frankl were dying everyday. By his own confession, he, too, was rapidly losing hope. His body grew weaker day by day and his ability to cope deteriorated rapidly.

One morning when the guards came to arouse all the prisoners, he could hardly drag himself from his cot. Once on the edge of his bed, he tied his clothes on with bits of wire and wrapped his feet with string to keep his shoes from falling off. His guards gave him a crust of bread as he joined the other prisoners as they plodded across the frozen ground, headed for the mine fields. As Frankl walked, he felt he was literally going to fall over and die. During that dark moment that seemed like hours, he mustered enough mental and emotional energy to think about his approach to helping others cope with suffering. Over the years, he had developed a philosophy of counseling he identified as logotherapy. For Frankl, this concept meant to help others "see meaning" in pain and suffering.

What meaning could Frankl possibly see in what was happening to him? As they trudged along, struggling between life and death, he was able to picture himself lecturing in an auditorium filled with people. He was speaking on the subject of "logotherapy" and how he had survived a Nazi concentration camp by practicing the principles embodied in this approach to enduring incredible weakness and pain and not giving up when every fiber in your mind and body is crying out to do so! The only meaning he could think of at that time was to be able to stand before this crowd of people and share with them that his therapy worked.

By being able to project in his mind this possibility, Frankl gained enough courage and strength to make it through the day. He then made it through another day and another—until the war was over and he was released.

I love to tell the rest of the story. A number of years ago, my wife and I attended a lecture at the University of Dallas. The guest speaker was none other than Victor Frankl. Though I had read the account of his experience earlier in one of his books, what a moment of awe to hear him share the story from his own lips. What he had seen in his mind's eye—which gave him strength to endure the suffering—was being lived out before our very eyes. There he stood, lecturing on the subject of how he endured the ravages of a Nazi concentration camp by seeing this particular meaning in his suffering—the opportunity to tell *us* about it. We were privileged to be a part of the "audience" in his mind!

As I sat and listened to Dr. Frankl, my heart was deeply moved. Here was a man who at that dark moment in his life did not claim to embrace the teachings of Jesus Christ—that He was the Messiah. However, he had discovered a very important principle that Jesus taught—a principle that worked even for him. He was able to believe that "good" could come from this terrible experience precipitated by the very embodiment of evil—Hitler himself.

As I reflected on Dr. Frankl's experience, I thought of Joseph's encouraging words to his brothers—"'You intended to harm me, but God intended it for good'" (50:20). I also thought of this great truth as expressed by Paul in Romans 8:28. I concluded that if this principle will work for those who do not claim to be Christians, then what about those of us who really do know Jesus Christ as personal Lord and Savior? How much more should *we* be able to see meaning in suffering—even though we may not be able to understand its ultimate purpose?

Personalizing These Principles

What we believe about God and His involvement in our lives should make a difference as to how we face difficult circumstances. We're all human beings, just like Joseph. And even though God had a very unusual and special purpose for allowing suffering in his life, we can also apply the truth in Romans 8:28—"And we know that in all things God works for the good of those who love him, who have been called according to his purpose."

Set a Goal

Today you may be suffering—either because of your own sinful actions or because of the sinful actions of others. As you review the principles in this chapter that relate to suffering, what specific lesson can you apply immediately to your own life? Turn this particular lesson into a personal goal:

_____

_____

_____

_____

Memorize the Following Scripture

And we know that in all things God works for the good of those who love him, who have been called according to his purpose.
ROMANS 8:28

Growing Together

The following questions are designed for small group discussion:

1. What experiences have you had where you've suffered deeply but now see God's purpose in this suffering? Would you be willing to share both the experience and the purpose?

2. What painful experience are you having right now, but you can't see any particular purpose in this suffering?

3. As a Christian, think about Victor Frankl's experience. Is there some way to identify some meaning in your suffering that you've not been able to think of before?

4. How can we pray for you particularly?

Endnotes

Chapter 1

1. To check the accuracy of this first-person account that focuses primarily on Joseph's father, Jacob, read Genesis 25:19–35:29. Also consult the author's book in this *Men of Character* series entitled *Jacob: Following God without Looking Back* (Nashville: Broadman & Holman Publishers, 1996).

Chapter 2

1. See *The Measure of a Man* by Gene A. Getz which was completely rewritten and released by Regal Books in 1995. This book devotes twenty chapters to the qualities outlined by Paul in 1 Timothy and Titus.

Chapter 3

1. To understand more fully the basis of this theory, consult the study on Jacob's life in this men's series by Gene A. Getz, *Jacob: Following God Without Looking Back* (Nashville: Broadman & Holman Publishers, 1995).

Chapter 5

1. You can calculate Joseph's age at this juncture with two specific references. He was seventeen when Jacob made him his royal robe (Gen. 37:2). He was thirty when he became prime minister of

Egypt (Gen. 41:46). And the events in chapter 40 took place two years before he became prime minister (Gen. 41:1).

2. Corrie ten Boom, *Tramp for the Lord* (Old Tappan, N.J.: Fleming H. Revell Co., 1974), 55–57. Reprinted by permission from *Guideposts* magazine, copyright 1972 by Guideposts Associates, Inc., Carmel, New York 10512.

Chapter 6

1. Corrie ten Boom, *Tramp for the Lord* (Old Tappan, N.J.: Fleming H. Revell Co., 1974), 23–24. Reprinted by permission.

Chapter 7

1. Aiden W. Tozer, *Root of the Righteous* (Harrisburg, Pa.: Christian Publications, Inc., nd), 137.

Chapter 8

1. Consult the author's books entitled *Building Up One Another, Loving One Another, Encouraging One Another, Praying for One Another—* all published by Victor Books, Wheaton, Illinois.

Chapter 9

1. Corrie ten Boom, *Tramp for the Lord,* 181–83. Reprinted by permission.

Chapter 10

1. Alfred Edersheim, *Old Testament Bible History* (Grand Rapids: Wm. B. Eerdmans Publishing Company, 1977), 168.